A Little Lower
than the Angels

David W. Christner

MOONFLOWER PRESS

DEDICATION

This play is for oppressed people everywhere and especially for Bunmi, Marc, Pamela, Sylvia and Eddie Jackson.

CONTENTS

A LITTLE LOWER THAN THE ANGELS

CAST OF CHARACTERS

AUCTIONEER (voice).................Doubled

ADAM JEFFERSON.....................21, a Virginia born slave

JOHN RUTLEDGE......................33, Southern planter

CHARLES RUTLEDGE. ....23, John's brother

CONSTANCE CLARKE..............23, Charles' fiancée

SOPHIA...18, a Carolina born slave

THOMAS CLARKE ....44, Constance's father

MARIA PIRES ....40, a sailmaker

The Setting

Area set includes a sitting room in Newport, a sail loft, a bedroom, an auction block, a cliff overlooking the ocean, an office, the after-deck of a sloop, and a dueling site.

The Time

1803-1804—Newport, RI, at sea, and Charleston, SC.

Playwright's Notes

The characters and events in this play are fictional; however, the major role that Rhode Island played in the slave trade between 1725 and 1807 is a historical fact. During the period, the infamous trade triangle of Newport distilled rum for African slaves for West Indies molasses and sugar was a vital component of RI's economy. The "Guinea" trade as it was called resulted in the enslavement of 106,000 Africans; after the Revolutionary War ended, the trade was revived. As pointed out by scholar Jay Coughtry, in *The Notorious Triangle*, the "'American slave trade' might better be termed the 'Rhode Island slave trade'." This play is a dramatization of how that trade might have influenced the lives of a handful of early American patriots and their "property."

NOTICE

A LITTLE LOWER THAN THE ANGELS

by

David W. Christner

ACT I, SCENE I

SCENE:

A SPOTLIGHT COMES UP on ADAM JEFFERSON, 21, an A-American slave, who is standing on an auction block downstage center. As the white hot spot intensifies on Adam, we hear a voice.

VOICE (off).

O LORD, our Lord, how excellent is thy name in all the earth! who hast set thy glory above the heavens. [3] When I consider thy heavens, the work of thy fingers, the moon and the stars, which thou hast ordained; [4] What is man, that thou art mindful of him? and the son of man, that thou visitest him? [5] For thou hast made him a little lower than the angels, and hast crowned him with glory and honour.

(Adam is ruggedly handsome, muscular and stripped to the waist. In spite of the circumstances, he shows a strong resolve and quiet dignity. He was born into slavery in Virginia and has come to expect the worst. He has a rebellious streak, which is why he is being sold, and his back shows the scars of many beatings. He stands motionless under the spot, awaiting his fate.)

AUCTIONEER (off). Gentlemen, please, surely you can do better than that. What we have here is a prime specimen, young and strong. Good teeth, strong bones, trained to respect the whip. Take a look for yourself. This African is a number one slave—20 years old, strong as a bull, obedient and well on his way to becoming a skilled blacksmith. Now do I hear 400?

VOICE (off). Four hundred!

AUCTIONEER (off). I have 400. Do I hear 450?

VOICE (off). Four-fifty.

AUCTIONEER (off). Four-fifty! Do I hear 500?

VOICE (off). Five hundred!

VOICE (off). Six!

AUCTIONEER (off). Six hundred! Gentlemen, please. Don't make me beg. Six hundred is a steal for a specimen like this. If only used for breeding stock, he is worth twice that. This one speaks English as well as you or me, if you can get him to speak at all. Virginia born is he. Do I hear seven?

VOICE (off).   Seven!

VOICE (off).   Seven-fifty.

VOICE (off).   Eight hundred!

VOICE (off).   Eight-fifty!

(There is a moment of silence. The man looks out into the audience as if they are the bidders.)

AUCTIONEER (off). Don't quit on me now gentlemen. This slave can do the work of two men for the next 15—maybe 20 years. You will not find a slave of this quality anywhere between Newport and Havana. Do I hear 900?

VOICE (off).   Nine hundred.

AUCTIONEER (off). I have 900! Do I hear a thousand?

JOHN (off).   Twelve hundred dollars!

AUCTIONEER (off). Mercy, gentleman! Is that the best you can do? Twelve hundred dollars. That is a steal. Do I hear twelve-fifty? (Silence.) Very well, then. Twelve hundred—going once, going twice . . . and sold to

3

Mr. John Rutledge for twelve
hundred dollars. Thank you, sir.

(JOHN RUTLEDGE, 33, a Southern planter and
businessman ENTERS with his younger brother,
CHARLES, 23. Both are wearing white linen suits; John is
carrying a walking stick. They approach Adam to examine
him; John pokes him with the stick here and there and
looks in his mouth to examine his teeth. Charles seems
uncomfortable with the whole affair although he goes
along with it. Adam tolerates this abuse, but he clearly
doesn't like it.)

JOHN.   The auctioneer was right; this
                        Negro would have been a steal at
                        twice the price. Look at that chest
                        and those arms—good breeding
                        stock indeed, this one. Team him
                        up with a good strong woman, and
                        you will get ten slaves for the price
                        of one. (To the auctioneer.) What's
                        this one called?

ADAM.   I be Adam.

JOHN (to Adam). Very good. (A beat.) Adam—go to that
                        man over there; he will feed you
                        and give you water. You want
                        food—water?

ADAM.   Not eat for two days.

JOHN.   Go with that man; he will take care of you.

(ADAM exits.)

CHARLES. John, you do not have the need of any more slaves.

JOHN. He is not for me, Charles. Your future father-in-law needs a good man for his stable—a blacksmith. You are to take him on to Newport.

CHARLES. John, slaves can no longer be brought into Rhode Island; the law forbids it. Nor is the child of a slave anymore born into slavery.

JOHN. Charles, these laws are meaningless. They do nothing more than appease the collective conscience of the abolitionists, who have no idea of what to do with Negroes once they are free.

CHARLES. I cannot deny there is some truth in that; however, there are laws that not only restrict the slave trade, but also expressly prohibit importation of slaves into Rhode Island.

JOHN. Charles, in spite of these laws, the trade remains a most profitable enterprise, and Thomas Clarke has

	assured me that I can transfer property of this sort without interference. If anyone bothers to inquire, which is very doubtful, tell him Adam is an indentured servant.
CHARLES.	Of course, a servant. (A beat.) So, I am to transport this—servant to Newport?
JOHN.	Along with the rest of Mr. Clarke's property. (A beat.) Hate to let that one go actually. Could use him here.
CHARLES.	For what?
JOHN.	I have acquired land, more land. Not in the low country for rice— higher ground, inland, for cotton. It is cotton that will make the South king. With the cotton gin here and the Yankee mills, we can expand our market to the whole of New England and ultimately abroad. And with you settling in Newport—
CHARLES.	What makes you think I will settle in Newport?
JOHN.	Why I cannot imagine you will be leaving your future wife any time

soon, and I know for a fact that she would not fit into our more genteel Southern society.

CHARLES.   Constance is a very adaptable and capable woman. She can fit in wherever she pleases.

JOHN.   That is exactly my point: that she would not be *pleased* to adapt to our way of life.

CHARLES.   Our ways are different; that is all. There is nothing left for me here in any case. It was always my intention to concentrate my business interests in New England.

JOHN.   Because Father left all his property to me?

CHARLES.   That is your birthright.

JOHN.   But father did provide for your education . . .

CHARLES.   So I could make my own way in the world.

JOHN.   And you have! A degree from Harvard College. And—and this family alliance with Clarke's of Newport. You have succeeded beyond even my greatest

7

expectations. And was I not
responsible for your introduction
to Constance?

CHARLES.

You were responsible for my
introduction to her father.

JOHN.

You would not have even known
she existed had it not been for my
business relationship with her
father.

CHARLES.

I would have found Constance if
she were on the far side of the
world. How very little you know of
true love, Brother.

JOHN.

You needn't cast a shadow on my
marriage, Charles.

CHARLES.

That was not my intent. (A beat.)
Dare I inquire of Charlotte's
whereabouts?

JOHN.

I would not advise it.

CHARLES.

Where is she?

JOHN.

Atlanta. But my wife's whereabouts
is no concern of yours.

CHARLES.

What is it this time, John—drink or
something worse?

JOHN.

Charles, let us just celebrate your good fortune . . . not . . . dwell on the unfortunate consequences of my union with Charlotte.

CHARLES.

Brother, because she has not given you an heir is no reason to treat her so appallingly. And perhaps her inability to conceive is not—her fault alone.

JOHN.

That is not your affair! What matter is it to you how I treat her? If I have no heir, all the Rutledge holdings will someday be yours. That is in father's will, and I cannot change it.

CHARLES.

But you would no doubt like to.

JOHN.

Don't be difficult, little brother. For it is through my artifice that your success now *seems* assured.

CHARLES.

John, you must understand that prior to my engagement—in fact, before I even met her, I had already established a foundation on which to build my own career. You would be mistaken to assume that the Clarke fortune is a factor in my love for Constance.

JOHN.

Even so, you cannot deny that this alliance is a great convenience and a great boon to our mutual business interests.

CHARLES.

It is not a marriage of convenience, John, but one of deep and abiding love. I would love this woman even if she were a pauper.

JOHN.

Then thank God she is not for you too would be pauper in due course; for from what I can surmise, you could not live without her.

CHARLES.

I am not ashamed to admit it. In any case, if I can add your damned Rutledge cotton to the Clarke shipping list, it will only serve to secure my future and that of my wife to be!

JOHN.

You needn't be angry with me. I wish nothing but the best for you and your bride.

CHARLES.

Only because my success will ensure yours as well.

JOHN.

How can you be so cynical when I have arranged for such a special wedding gift for you and Constance?

CHARLES.   What is this special wedding gift?

JOHN.   You shall see in good time. (A beat.) Now, I have crops to harvest and you must catch the next high tide or be delayed another day from seeing your beloved.

CHARLES.   You are right, Brother. I must get underway.

(They shake hands a little awkwardly and John starts off.)

JOHN (turning back). I have new business with Thomas Clarke; I want to approach him about the use of the Slater Mill for my cotton. But I will refrain from mentioning your use of his daughter.

CHARLES.   Do not make me strike you, Brother. Another remark like that and I will miss the tide just to give you a good beating.

JOHN.   Charles, when did you ever beat me at anything?

CHARLES.   Brother, you are ten years my senior, and were of much larger stature in my youth. Now we are more evenly matched.

11

JOHN.   You will always wish it were so,
                         Brother. But we both know better.
                         Even so, I wish you well on your
                         voyage home. Good day, sir.

    (LIGHTS COME DOWN SLOWLY as Charles
        watches his brother walk away. He shakes
        his head in anger, then turns and exits.)

ACT I, SCENE II

SCENE: LIGHTS   COME   UP   on
                   CONSTANCE CLARKE, 23, in the
                   living room of a colonial Newport
                   home a week later. She is attractive
                   and bright, a schoolteacher, and from
                   one of Newport's wealthiest and
                   most respected families. She is pacing
                   about anxiously, waiting for Charles;
                   she is made up and dressed in the
                   fashion of the period. Upon hearing a
                   knock on the door, she rushes to
                   open it and is disappointed.

CONSTANCE.   Oh, Father . . . come in.

(THOMAS CLARKE, 55, ENTERS. He is a wealthy and
highly respected Newport merchant and community
leader. He is on the board of Trinity Church and a
Revolutionary War hero. He is an entrepreneur and has
established a far-reaching business empire, which stretches
from the west coast of Africa to Europe and the West
Indies.)

THOMAS.   You need not be so enthusiastic, Constance.

CONSTANCE.   I am sorry, Father, it's just that I was expecting—

THOMAS.   Someone else?

CONSTANCE.   Charles.

THOMAS.   I am well aware of that, and he will be here within the hour. The *Providence* just made Brenton Point and will be dockside momentarily.

CONSTANCE.   Father, I hope you do not think that I am in need of a chaperone to reacquaint myself with my husband to be.

THOMAS.   No, in fact I have made arrangements to dine out this evening. That is not why I have come.

CONSTANCE (after a moment). Very well. Why did you come?

THOMAS.   It is about—this wedding gift from John Rutledge.

CONSTANCE.   We have not yet received a gift from John.

THOMAS.   Indeed, you have. The—gift was delivered to my office this very afternoon.

CONSTANCE. Yes . . . and?

THOMAS. Did you know about it?

CONSTANCE. Charles wrote me that a gift was coming.

THOMAS. But not what?

CONSTANCE. No.

THOMAS. Did Charles know?

CONSTANCE. Only that a gift was coming. It was to be a surprise.

THOMAS. That it is, my dear. *That* it is.

CONSTANCE. A surprise. (A beat.) Well—those are invariably the best gifts of all.

THOMAS. One would like to think that.

CONSTANCE. But that is not the case in this instance?

THOMAS. I suppose that is a matter of opinion.

CONSTANCE. Then perhaps you should let me form my own.

THOMAS. You have always been free to do that, Constance, and woe be it to those who would keep you from it.

CONSTANCE.   Did you bring the gift home, or do
I have to venture to the wharf to
retrieve it?

THOMAS.   The—gift—is in my carriage.

CONSTANCE.   Shall I get it?

THOMAS.   No, please—sit. I will see to it.

(Thomas goes to the door, opens it, and motions to someone. Then he turns back to Constance, forces a smile and holds the door open. SOPHIA, 18, a Negro slave from South Carolina ENTERS. She is bright and confident; she has learned how to adapt and how to best survive. She has a firm grasp on the English language, having been raised in the household of the Rutledge plantation. Constance stands, looks at her, assuming the worst—that she has been given a slave as a wedding present—and then falls back in her chair.)

CONSTANCE.   Father, please tell me that what I
am thinking cannot be true.

THOMAS.   Constance, if you are thinking that
this Negro is given to you as a
wedding gift, then I cannot in truth
tell you anything different.
Although for legal purposes, I think
it best that she be referred to as an
indentured servant.

(Thomas takes a document from his coat.)

THOMAS.   This is a deed.

CONSTANCE.   This cannot be!

THOMAS.   Until your wedding, it will be
                 Charles who actually owns her.
                 After that, perhaps joint ownership
                 can be legally obtained if that is
                 what you desire.

CONSTANCE.   It is most certainly *not* what I
                 desire. I will not have a slave in my
                 house.

THOMAS.   This is my house, Constance.

CONSTANCE.   And I have run it since Mother
                 died!

THOMAS.   When your house is complete, you
                 can take her there and do with her
                 what you will. It is not my concern.

CONSTANCE.   I will not have a slave in my house!

THOMAS.   You made that point previously.
                 And I was quite certain that those
                 are the exact sentiments you would
                 express, however, it is not my role
                 any longer to advise you of such
                 difficult matters.

CONSTANCE.   I seek no advice. All I request is
                 that, if need be, this woman can be
                 housed under your roof until such
                 time that her position . . . can be
                 clarified.

THOMAS.   She may, of course, be housed in
                 the garret with the household staff
                 until such time that—you and

17

	Charles decide what is to become of her. Now, I must take my leave. Charles will be here straight away, and I . . . don't want to get in the way of your reunion. (A beat.) Shall I take the girl?
CONSTANCE.	No, she can stay.
THOMAS.	You cannot escape from here. You are on an island.
CONSTANCE.	You will not be mistreated here.
THOMAS.	She was not mistreated on the way here, but I understand she tried twice to escape.
SOPHIA.	Three times. (A beat. Then to Constance.) I will not run away, ma'am.
CONSTANCE.	Do I have your word?
SOPHIA.	Yes, ma'am. You have my word.
THOMAS.	I must take my leave.
CONSTANCE.	Good evening, Father.

THOMAS (exiting). Good evening, Constance.

CONSTANCE (turning to Sophia). Please, sit.

SOPHIA.	Oh, no ma'am, can't sit if you're standin'.

CONSTANCE.   You can in this house. Please, sit.
                   (A beat.) I shall sit too. (They both
                   sit.) Well . . . do you know where
                   you are?

SOPHIA.   I know the name of where I am—
                   Newport in the State of Rhode
                   Island and Providence
                   Plantations—but jist zakly where
                   that is, I don't rightly know.

CONSTANCE.   It is hundreds of miles north of
                   South Carolina—where you came
                   from.

SOPHIA.   Charleston.

CONSTANCE.   Yes—Charleston. Do you know
                   why you are here?

SOPHIA.   'Cuse me for saying so, ma'am, but
                   I don't worry much 'bout "why". I
                   jist do what's expected of me. Less
                   trouble that way.

CONSTANCE.   My god! (A beat.) You know, here
                   in New England, the institution of
                   slavery is—

SOPHIA.   Is what, ma'am?

CONSTANCE.   Is—practiced to a—lesser extent
                   than in the South.

SOPHIA.   I see, ma'am—"a lesser extent."

CONSTANCE.   Do you know what that means?

SOPHIA (thinks, then pointedly). Do you?

CONSTANCE.   You are very bright, but you must know that.

SOPHIA.   Does that surprise you?

CONSTANCE.   No. It does not. I teach in a school for Negro children; given an equal opportunity for learning, I have found that there is no difference in the learning capacity of Negro children and the children of European descent. (A beat.) I suppose what I was trying to tell you is that in New England we have—far fewer people in positions of subservience than in South Carolina.

SOPHIA.   Why is that, ma'am?

CONSTANCE.   Well, I suppose it is because—we have less of a need for—laborers.

SOPHIA.   I see, but, on my trip here, all the people I saw working the fields were dark skinned

CONSTANCE.   In any case, you will not be a slave in any house of mine.

SOPHIA.   Do you have a house, ma'am?

CONSTANCE.   No, but I will within the year— after I marry. This house belongs to my father, Thomas Clarke, the man that brought you here.

SOPHIA. He is—very kind.

CONSTANCE. Yes, he is. And a pillar of the community. For a wedding gift, he is building a house for my future husband and me.

SOPHIA. I am a wedding gift too, that right? From Massa John?

CONSTANCE. What is your name?

SOPIHIA. Sophia.

CONSTANCE. Sophia, I am Constance Elizabeth Clarke, and I will not accept another human being as a gift. I do not want you to think of yourself as—my property.

SOPHIA. Then will I be the property of your husband?

CONSTANCE. That may have to be the case until this affair is settled. Now, I must receive my fiancée and I am sure you want to freshen up after your trip. There is a guest room through that door; you will find everything you need. I will speak with Charles when he arrives and then call for you.

SOPHIA. Thank you, ma'am.

CONSTANCE.   Please don't call me that; you are not a child.

SOPHIA.   All right—Miss Constance. I will wait for you to call.

(SOPHIA exits. Constance begins pacing. She goes to the window, pulls back the curtain and peers out. Finally, she sits down on the edge of the couch and picks up a copy of the *Newport Mercury*.)

CHARLES (off).   Constance. Constance!

(Constance jumps off the couch and rushes to the door as Charles begins pounding. She flings the door open and CHARLES enters. They embrace and kiss passionately like the lovers they are.)

CHARLES.   Constance. My beautiful Constance. How I have missed you.

CONSTANCE.   And I you.

CHARLES.   Oh my sweetness, I have ached for your touch.

CONSTANCE.   As have I ached for yours.

CHARLES.   I must have you—here—now. Is your father about?

CONSTANCE.   No, I made him promise to give us a few hours, but—Charles . . .

(He picks her up and heads for the door
leading to her bedroom.)

CHARLES.   No protests, my love, I have been
without you too long.

CONSTANCE.   Charles, wait. There is something
we have to discuss.

CHARLES.   We can have a discussion later.

CONSTANCE.   This is a matter of great urgency.

CHARLES (kisses her). So is this!

CONSTANCE.   Charles, no! Put me down.

(He puts her down on the couch.)

CHARLES.   Very well, my dear, if you have a
matter of greater urgency than my
desire for you, then I must
accommodate you for a moment—
but *only* for a moment.

CONSTANCE (fixing her dress, etc.). Would you care for
some spirits?

CHARLES.   You know what I'd care for.

CONSTANCE.   Charles, please.

CHARLES.   No spirits. Just get on with it.

CONSTANCE (pouring him a drink). I think you should
have some spirits.

CHARLES (staring at her). My god you are beautiful,
Constance. And what I ever did to
deserve your love I do not know.

23

Just one more kiss—before you go on.

(They kiss again; Constance is on the very edge of giving in as Charles maneuvers her to a reclining position on the couch. THERE IS A KNOCKING ON AN INTERIOR DOOR. Constance jumps us, again fixing her dress.)

CHARLES. Who is that?

CONSTANCE. Yes?

(SOPHIA enters.)

CONSTANCE. Oh, Sophia . . .

SOPHIA. I have finished unpacking, Miss Constance. I was wonderin' if you might need help with something else.

CHARLES (from the couch).Who is Sophia?

CONSTANCE. Sophia is our wedding gift from your brother. *She* is what I wanted to talk to you about.

CHARLES (rises and sees her). Sophia? Sophia!

SOPHIA. Hello, Massa Charles.

CHARLES. Little Sophia?

CONSTANCE. You know this woman?

SOPHIA. We both growed some, Massa Charles.

CONSTANCE.   You know her!

CHARLES (hugging her). Sophia! How are you?

SOPHIA.   Much better now that I seen you.

CONSTANCE.   Do not ignore me, Charles.

CHARLES (to Sophia). Your family—are they—still . . . in
                  Charleston?

SOPHIA.   No, after the accident that took
                  your folks . . . everybody went
                  somewheres else.

CHARLES.   I am sorry for that, Sophia.

CONSTANCE.   What does she mean—"went
                  somewhere else?"

SOPHIA.   After you leave for schoolin'—you
                  never come back.

CHARLES.   After the accident, there was
                  nothing left for me down there.

SOPHIA.   I never forget those days.

CHARLES.   I guess I did. (A beat.) I am sorry
                  for that.

SOPHIA.   No fault of yours, Massa Charles.
                  You young and—

CHARLES.   Foolish. Now I am older—but
                  probably no less foolish. I should
                  have been there.

CONSTANCE.   Sophia, since my fiancée is ignoring me, would you please tell me what you two are talking about?

SOPHIA.   Old times, Miss Constance. Old times when Massa Charles and me was childrens.

CONSTANCE.   Charles?

CHARLES.   Sophia's family worked in the main house—cooking, cleaning, mending; her father was the gardener. Mattie, Sophia's mother, had as much to do with my upbringing as my own mother. She told us stories, and on days when she was working, she would have me read stories to Sophia. I was only ten; Sophia was five, but I kept it up until I left for college.

SOPHIA.   I jist becoming a woman then.

CHARLES.   The accident happened my first year at Harvard, and I never went back until I started working for your father.

SOPHIA.   It was Massa Charles taught me to read. Taught me lots of other things too.

CHARLES.   Did I ever get a beating for that!

CONSTANCE.   Well, maybe I should leave you two alone to catch up?

CHARLES.   Sophia, I feel terrible about what happened; maybe if I'd been there—

SOPHIA.   You couldn't of done nothin'. Massa John always did what he wanted.

CONSTANCE.   What did he do?

CHARLES.   He sold off Sophia's family.

CONSTANCE.   Good Lord! Sold them off . . .

SOPHIA.   You own me now, Massa Charles. You and Miss Constance.

CONSTANCE.   We will never *own* you, Sophia.

CHARLES.   No, not in a philosophical sense, but in a very real legal sense, we do or will jointly when we marry.

CONSTANCE.   Charles, we have to return her.

CHARLES.   To what? She would be much worse off there.

CONSTANCE.   Then we will free her.

CHARLES.   Of course, when it is most advantageous to do so.

CONSTANCE.   Advantageous to whom?

CHARLES.   Sophia.

CONSTANCE.   How can keeping her in bondage a
              second longer be of any advantage
              to her?

CHARLES.   Sophia, would you excuse us?

SOPHIA.   Yes, Massa Charles. I very tired.
              Won't be botherin' you and Miss
              Constance again. I know you gots
              lots to catch up on.

CHARLES.   Thank you, Sophia.

CONSTANCE.   Have you had something to eat?

SOPHIA.   I fine, Miss. I jist retire for the
              evening now. Good night.

CONSTANCE   Good night.

(SOPHIA exits. Charles crosses to Constance and takes
her in his arms. She breaks away.)

CONSTANCE.   I am in no mood for that now.

CHARLES.   Constance, you are not going to let
              a—Sophia come between us.

CONSTANCE.   A slave? Were you going to say, "a
              slave?" (He doesn't answer.) I think
              Charles that perhaps I do not know
              you as well as I thought.

CHARLES.   Constance, I did not return to
              Charleston after my education
              because I chose not to participate
              in that way of life.

CONSTANCE.   And yet you still find yourself a
              slave owner.

CHARLES.   Through no fault of mine! And is
              this household not run with
              indentured servants? Tell me,
              Constance; is there such a great
              difference?

CONSTANCE.   Let me enlighten you about the
              practice of slavery in Rhode Island.
              A child can no longer be born into
              bondage in this state, nor is it legal
              for the slave trade to be carried on
              by ships from any of Rhode
              Island's ports.

CHARLES.   But is it not illegal to *own* slaves.
              And while these laws address the
              institution of slavery, they do little to
              limit the practice of it. Even the
              post-nati manumission acts require
              the children of slaves to remain in
              servitude until they reach majority.

CONSTANCE.   The laws are not yet perfect, but
              they are a beginning. This matter is
              greatly complicated by the fact that
              slaves are considered property, and
              if—

CHARLES.   Constance, can you not put this
              issue aside for a few hours? I beg
              you.

CONSTANCE.   It will not go away of its own
              accord, Charles.

CHARLES (takes her hand). I know that, Darling, so why can we not address it just as well in a few hours or on another day? Do you not long for me as much as I long for you?

CONSTANCE (weakening). Charles, I have missed you desperately. You must know that from my letters.

CHARLES (kisses her tenderly). I do know that, Love. Will you not allow me to take away some of your longing without any further delay?

CONSTANCE. Charles, it very important that you understand where I stand.

CHARLES (kisses her more passionately). Tomorrow you can tell me where you stand. Tonight I think it more important for us to come to an understanding in a horizontal position. Agreed?

CONSTANCE. Yes, my love. Agreed.

(They kiss passionately as the LIGHTS COME DOWN TO END THE SCENE.)

ACT I, SCENE III

SCENE: LIGHTS COMES UP on THOMAS
                       working in an office overlooking the
                       docks in Newport. After a moment,
                       there is a knock at the door. Thomas
                       looks up as Charles ENTERS.

THOMAS.   Ah, Charles, come in, come in, my
                       boy.

CHARLES.   Thank you, Sir.

THOMAS.   Good to have you home.

CHARLES.   It is most gratifying to be back, Sir.

THOMAS.   I trust that everything went well
                       with your reunion with my
                       daughter.

CHARLES.   Yes, I am pleased to report that it
                       was a success. Thank you, Sir.

Although things did not go quite as smoothly as I had anticipated.

THOMAS.   Because of the slave girl?

CHARLES.   Yes, Sophia's arrival did provoke some concern on Constance's part.

THOMAS.   Well, in any case, I know she is well satisfied to have you back home.

CHARLES.   I certainly hope that is the case.

THOMAS.   I have just now completed my review of the accounts for this voyage, and I am pleased to say that it was a great success for me as well as my investors—thanks to you. Had you not been willing to complete the voyage from Barbados, things might have turned out quite differently. I thank you.

CHARLES.   The loss of Captain Ambrose had to have been quite a startling blow.

THOMAS.   These things are quite common in the trade. Nasty business. And I will see to it personally that his family is well provided for.

CHARLES.   I have no reason to doubt that you will do what is right by his family. What was it exactly that . . . took Captain Ambrose?

THOMAS.   The fever—Malaria. He contracted
                 it . . . in the tropics—and never
                 quite recovered. You know how it
                 goes down there.

CHARLES.   Yes sir, I'm well aware of the perils
                 of the tropics. (A few beats.) I just
                 was not—

THOMAS.   Was not what, Son?

CHARLES.   Aware of what—region of the
                 tropics Captain Ambrose
                 contracted the disease. I'm
                 assuming it was in the West Indies.

THOMAS.   May I speak frankly, Son?

CHARLES.   Of course. I would expect nothing
                 less of you.

THOMAS.   Would it be a problem for you if—
                 say the disease had been contracted
                 further east?

CHARLES.   How far east?

THOMAS.   I think we both know how far.
                 (Silence.) Surely, Charles, having
                 been raised a Southern gentleman,
                 this will not present a problem for
                 you?

CHARLES (after a moment). No sir, of course not, but I
                 fear that my relationship with
                 Constance could come under close
                 scrutiny if she—

THOMAS.   Constance knows very little of my business affairs. My investors and I finance her school for Negro children, and that gives her time for little else. My participation in the trade, along with that of my investors, is not something that we desire to come under public or private scrutiny. And this—African trade is not by any means the only commerce I conduct.

CHARLES.   But it is the most profitable.

THOMAS.   As any Southern gentleman would well know. Is that not the case? Or did I misread you?

CHARLES.   I do not know what you read, Sir, but that is indeed the case.

THOMAS.   Excellent. (A beat.) And did you not return from Charleston with property for me?

CHARLES.   I did. (A beat.) He is just outside.

THOMAS.   Call him.

CHARLES (going to door). Adam!

(ADAM enters.)

THOMAS.   Come over here.

CHARLES.   Adam, this is—

ADAM.   Massa Thomas. I knows all about
                         him already; his—servants tell me
                         last night. He a good man, they say.
                         Fair and just, hardly ever beats 'em.

CHARLES.   He is a good man.

ADAM.   Adam a good man too.

THOMAS.   Which Adam?

ADAM.   From the Bible—the first man.

THOMAS.   Indeed, he was a good man. As I
                         have no doubt you will be as well.

CHARLES.   You will not be mistreated here,
                         Adam.

THOMAS.   And you will have a great deal more
                         freedom here than you had in
                         South Carolina. There are no
                         overseers in my stables.

ADAM.   I was lived in Virginia; jist got sold
                         down to South Carolina.

THOMAS.   No one will be—standing over you
                         every minute of the day. You will
                         do your work at the stables, and
                         then you will be free to do as you
                         please—within reason. For obvious
                         reasons, we must maintain some—
                         night patrols. (A beat.) What do
                         you know about horses, Adam?

ADAM.   I know the rear end of one when I
                         sees it.

THOMAS.   Charles, did he just—

CHARLES.   Adam, let me take you down to the stables now. Sidney will show you the shop and tell you what is expected of you.

THOMAS.   And introduce him to that girl of yours.

CHARLES.   Sophia?

THOMAS.   Indeed. Good stock—the two of them.

CHARLES.   Come with me, Adam.

ADAM.   Yes sir; ain't got nothin' planned jist now anyway.

THOMAS.   Take some time off, Charles. You well deserve it. We can catch up on business affairs in a few days. If I start taking all your time, I will have to bear the wrath of my daughter. We shall just let the winds of Fate determine the time and place of our next business venture.

(LIGHTS COME DOWN SLOWLY
as Charles and Adam exit.)

ACT I, SCENE IV

SCENE: LIGHTS COME UP on SOPHIA
                        and ADAM a week later. They are
                        in the sitting room of Thomas
                        Clarke's home. Sophia is carrying a
                        shopping basket under one arm.

ADAM.   Miss Sophia, I was told by Massa
                        Charles to escort you to wherever it
                        is you needs to go. And that's what
                        I intends to do.

SOPHIA.   What if I needs to go do my private
                        business?

ADAM.   Then I be goin' right along with
                        you. That foe sure.

SOPHIA.   You most surely won't! (A beat.)
                        Now let me check my list.

ADAM.   What's that?

SOPHIA.   A list of things Miss Constance needs from the market.

ADAM (pointing to list). What's that right there?

SOPHIA.   Oil.

ADAM.   Oil?

SOPHIA.   Whale oil for the lamps. We gotta have some light in the house at night. (A beat.) You don't read, do you Adam?

ADAM.   No one never taught me. I can make my mark though. (A beat.) Where'd you learn; slaves ain't sposed to read—against the law.

SOPHIA.   Massa Charles teach me—back in Charleston when we was both jist childrens. Taught me rithmatic too. Got a awful beatin' for it, he did.

ADAM.   Who from?

SOPHIA.   Massa John—big brother. You right; Massa John didn't much cotton to the idea of slaves readin', no sir.

ADAM.   Maybe . . . sometime you could teach . . . me—

SOPHIA.   Teach you to read?

ADAM.   Wouldn't do no harm.

SOPHIA.   Adam, I would be most happy to
                   teach you to read.

ADAM.   Good. I thank you for that. Maybe
                   we can start tomorrow. Right now
                   though, I gotta gits you to the
                   market.

SOPHIA.   You don't gots to git me nowhere!

ADAM.   Massa Charles said!

SOPHIA.   You always do what your Massa
                   says?

ADAM.   Most surely do.

SOPHIA.   You don't! If you did, you wouldn't
                   have . . . all those scars on your
                   back.

ADAM.   Oh, so you been lookin' at Adam's
                   back.

SOPHIA.   I saw you down at the stables; I
                   wasn't lookin'. You weren't hiding
                   anythin' either—no shirt on.
                   Beatin' on that anvil with a big
                   hammer. What a sight that was.

ADAM.   Got nothin' to hide. In fact—got
                   nothin' at all. Neither does you.

SOPHIA.   Oh, I got plenty—plenty—

ADAM.   Plenty of nothin'!

SOPHIA.   You don't know what I got.

ADAM.   I knows one thing you got.

SOPHIA.   What's that?

ADAM.   Oh, I think you knows what I'm
                     talkin' bout.

SOPHIA.   Why Adam—what's your family
                     name, Adam? I don't even know.

ADAM.   Jefferson. Least that the name we
                     took. Belonged to Massa Jefferson
                     in Virginia.

SOPHIA.   You not talkin' 'bout Thomas
                     Jefferson?

ADAM.   Most surely am.

SOPHIA.   You was owned by the President of
                     the United States?

ADAM.   Most surely was.

SOPHIA (thinks, then). Well . . . Massa Charles' father,
                     John Rutledge, Senior—he signed
                     the Declaration of Independence,
                     he did.

ADAM.   Massa Jefferson done went and
                     wrote the thing!

SOPHIA.   Ain't that somethin'? We both been
                     owned by some of the finest men
                     in the entire country. (A beat.)
                     Adam, how come Massa Jefferson
                     sell you off like that?

ADAM.   Massa Jefferson never would of
               sold me off; he went off to be
               President. Foreman sold me; said I
               be a troublemaker. Massa Jefferson
               never knowed nothin' 'bout it.

SOPHIA.   Or maybe he gots more important
               things on his mind now?

ADAM.   Not to *me*, he don't.

SOPHIA.   Well, in any case Adam Jefferson, I
               jist wants you to know this one
               thing—

ADAM.   'Fore you start scoldin' me, why
               don't you ask me what I was talkin'
               'bout before?

SOPHIA.   All right, Adam Jefferson, I will.
               What is the one thing I got that you
               know I got?

ADAM.   My—heartfelt affection.

SOPHIA (surprised and flattered). Oh, why—I had—no
               idea 'bout that. I hadn't done
               nothin'—l

ADAM.   You didn't havta do nothin'. Jist—
               bein' there was nuff.

SOPHIA.   Bein' where?

ADAM.   The stables!

SOPHIA.   I declare—

41

ADAM.

And why in the world you think I be over here every spare minute I got? You thinks I *really* likes to go to *market*? Market ain't no place foe a man to be goin'.

SOPHIA.

Oh . . .

ADAM.

And, if I not mistaken, you spendin' a whole lot more time down at the stables than you really needs to.

SOPHIA.

What do you mean by that Adam Jefferson?

ADAM.

What do you mean by bein' down there all the time?

SOPHIA.

I there to tend to Miss Constance's mare; she sends me down with carrots and sugar.

ADAM.

Sugar? You feedin' that sorry nag sugar that could better be used to make rum! You most surely are headed for trouble, girl.

SOPHIA.

Rum?

ADAM.

Girl. You been livin' in a cave? What you think they do with that sugar and molasses comes up on Massa Tom's ships?

SOPHIA.

Don't know; ain't none of my affair.

ADAM.   Guinea rum! They makes the rum
                        here that gets traded for slaves in
                        Africa.

SOPHIA.   Adam, you takin' nonsense now.
                        These people treat us good; they
                        not slavers. We practically free
                        here.

ADAM.   Yeah, we free all right—free to do
                        what we gotta do. You do good,
                        boy, you get treated jist fine. You
                        do bad, you gits punished. Jist like
                        you treat a dog. You rise up and
                        bite your master, they take an shoot
                        you. No different here than down
                        there; they jist don't like to see it
                        that way. Calls us servants instead
                        of slaves—ain't no difference that I
                        can see.

SOPHIA.   But they gonna free us; Miss
                        Constance said so.

ADAM (bitterly). Only one-way we ever gonna be free.

SOPHIA.   Adam, don't talk like that. I gotta
                        git free. I gotta . . .

ADAM.   I sorry, Miss Sophia. I jist gots so
                        much anger inside of me
                        sometimes . . . jist wants to choke
                        the first white man I sees.

SOPHIA (touches his face). I know you do; but it is better
                        here, Adam. At least—

ADAM (taking her hand). 'Least what?

SOPHIA.   Least we can see each other if we have a notion.

ADAM.   That mean you wants to?

SOPHIA.   It might . . . jist don't be gittin' any ideas.

ADAM.   Well, I wants to see you; wants to see you all the time, Miss Sophia. Sometimes I feel like I'm gonna bust if I can't just take you in my arms . . .

SOPHIA.   Why don't you then? Don't wanna see you bust.

(He takes her in his arms tentatively and then he kisses her very tenderly, as if it is his first time. As they embrace, the door opens and CHARLES and CONSTANCE enter. Adam and Sophia break away.)

CONSTANCE.   Oh . . . Sophia.

CHARLES.   Adam . . . you were to take Sophia to market.

ADAM.   Yes sir, Mr. Charles. We headed there right now. We jist—

SOPHIA.   Gittiin' better acquainted.

CHARLES.   I can see that you are.

SOPHIA.   We goin' right now, Miss Constance.

(They start out.)

CONSTANCE.   Sophia?

SOPHIA.   Yes ma'am.

CONSTANCE.   You forgot your shopping basket.

SOPHIA.   Yes ma'am. Thank you ma'am.

(SOPHIA and ADAM exit.)

CHARLES.   Well, I suppose we shall have to keep a tighter rein on those two.

CONSTANCE.   Why?

CHARLES.   Is the reason not obvious?

CONSTANCE.   What?

CHARLES.   The way they looked at each other. The fact that they were— embracing when we walked in.

CONSTANCE.   Charles—are you afraid that they might do as we have done?

CHARLES.   Well—I . . .

CONSTANCE.   Would you deny them love?

CHARLES.   Perhaps what we witnessed between them is something other than love?

CONSTANCE.   What if it is?

CHARLES.   Constance!

CONSTANCE.   Would you deny them a simple
                 pleasure, when they have so little of
                 it anywhere else?

CHARLES.   Constance, there are—
                 responsibilities that come with such
                 pleasures.

CONSTANCE.   I am well aware of that.

CHARLES.   But they have not the means to
                 fulfill such responsibilities.

CONSTANCE.   And where can the reason for that
                 be placed?

CHARLES.   Constance, my love, you lack a
                 fundamental understanding of the
                 African character.

CONSTANCE.   They were both born in the
                 colonies, Charles. They are as
                 American as either of us, so why do
                 you insist on calling them Africans?

CHARLES.   Whatever they are called is beside
                 the point. The fact remains that
                 you have no conception of their
                 makeup.

CONSTANCE.   Then enlighten me, please.

CHARLES.   Africans—Negroes—do not have
                 the—same capacity to care for
                 themselves as civilized people.

CONSTANCE (thinks, then). I see. But—didn't you tell me that you were practically raised by a Negro woman because of your mother's poor health.

CHARLES. That is true. I was, but that is different.

CONSTANCE. So, this Negro woman who raised you had the capacity to take care of you, and in all probability your mother, but not herself. Is that correct?

CHARLES. Yes. No. No! She could care for herself and me within the narrow limits of a—very stable physical environment.

CONSTANCE. Such as a plantation?

CHARLES. Yes, because there was a place for her there.

CONSTANCE. Of course there was—for as long as she knew her place. And God help her if she did not! Is that not the way it was on the plantation?

CHARLES. Constance, I pray you will not let the practice of slavery drive a wedge between us. I chose to pursue an education in New England to distance myself from that way of life. What I found, however, is that I simply exchanged the Southern variety of slavery for that which is practiced in the enlightened North. And if the truth be known, the difference in principle is insignificant. In any case, it was never my intention to hold people in bondage, here or in Charleston.

CONSTANCE.   And yet Sophia is your property, is she not?

CHARLES.   And does Adam not belong to your father?

CONSTANCE.   If I can get Father to free Adam, will you release Sophia?

CHARLES.   Release her to what?

CONSTANCE.   Should that not be for her to decide?

CHARLES.   Constance, even if Negroes are free, they are not—

CONSTANCE.   White?

CHARLES.   Like us. And I do not know if there is a place for free Africans here or anywhere else in New England. As her—owner, I am responsible for Sophia's welfare.

CONSTANCE.   You think she is incapable of caring for herself?

CHARLES.   It would be—very difficult.

48

CONSTANCE.   Charles, Sophia is an expert
              seamstress; she could work at a
              shop.

CHARLES.   What shop in Newport is going to
              take in a Negro? What shop in
              Newport is going to pay a Negro a
              wage?

CONSTANCE.   Then I will find work for her on
              the waterfront; surely a seamstress
              could be of great value to a sail-
              maker.

CHARLES.   Constance, Sophia's welfare is my
              responsibility. And she was sent
              here to be of service to you.

CONSTANCE.   I am not in need of her service.
              Charles, she has a right to live her
              own life. You must let her go.

CHARLES.   For better or for worse?

CONSTANCE.   An interesting choice of words,
              Charles.

CHARLES.   Show me that she can meet her
              own needs, and I will free her.

CONSTANCE.   I have your word.

CHARLES.   Constance, you have my
              everything. You know that.

CONSTANCE.   Sometimes I wonder.

CHARLES.   Ease your mind of that burden; you
                have no reason to wonder about
                my devotion to you. It is
                unconditional.

CONSTANCE.   It is just that I know so little of
                your business affairs; you work for
                my father, but insofar as business is
                concerned, you tell me nothing;
                you treat me as he does, as if I were
                a child—as if I have not the
                intellect to comprehend the world
                of commerce. Like you, Charles, I
                have an education and an
                inquisitive mind.

CHARLES.   I know that, Constance. And of
                course you could comprehend
                business; there is no mystery about
                it. But I would much prefer to talk
                with you about affairs of the heart
                rather than those of commerce.

CONSTANCE.   Are affairs of the heart so
                unrelentingly interesting to you?

CHARLES.   Are they not to you?

CONSTANCE.   I think perhaps it is something
                other than the heart that
                commands such unbridled
                enthusiasm on both our parts.

CHARLES.   Pray it will always remain so, my
                love.

CONSTANCE.   I do, Charles. I pray it will remain
                    so for all human beings who are
                    caught up in the fire of passion's
                    grip.

CHARLES.   Sophia and Adam?

CONSTANCE (kissing him). Us. Now—come with me
                    lest this smoldering fire consumes
                    us both.

(They exit as the LIGHTS COME DOWN SLOWLY.)

ACT I, SCENE V

SCENE: LIGHTS COME UP A WEEK LATER on MARIA PIRES, 30, a woman of color from the Cape Verdes. She makes sails in a loft owned by her husband who is off on a whaling voyage. There are piles of "canvas" scattered about the dimly lit room. She hears someone outside.

MARIA.   Who's there?

(CONSTANCE and SOPHIA ENTER.)

CONSTANCE.   Mrs. Pires?

MARIA.   I am Maria Pires. Yes—

CONSTANCE.   We came from the wharf—

MARIA.   That is the only way to get here; what do you want? I am busy.

CONSTANCE.   I am Constance Clarke; you have
               made many sails for my father's
               schooners and barks.

MARIA.   Thomas Clarke is your father?

CONSTANCE.   Yes.

MARIA.   Is he not satisfied with my work?

CONSTANCE.   He is very satisfied; he has no
               complaints.

MARIA.   Who is that?

CONSTANCE.   This is Sophia; she is why I am
               here.

MARIA.   I do not know her.

CONSTANCE.   She is an excellent seamstress; she
               needs work, and Captain Almy told
               me you needed help here.

MARIA.   Can you sew heavy canvass?

SOPHIA.   I don't know.

CONSTANCE.   She is very gifted.

MARIA.   Let me see your hands.

(Sophia holds out her hands for Maria to examine.)

MARIA.   You have done plenty hard work
               with these hands.

SOPHIA.   Yes—

MARIA.   You read?

SOPHIA.   Yes ma'am.

MARIA.   Measure? Know your numbers?

SOPHIA.   Yes ma'am.

MARIA.   No call me, Ma'am. I same color as
                    you. You call me Maria.

(Sophia nods.)

MARIA.   I pay you one dollar for every day.

CONSTANCE.   That is only six dollars a week.

MARIA.   Seven—work every day. No time
                    for rest like God; God got no need
                    for money. Maria need plenty—
                    never enough. Work ten hours
                    every day, Sunday too.

CONSTANCE.   Ten hours!

SOPHIA.   If I make sails good, you pay me
                    more?

MARIA.   You make them good—we see.

CONSTANCE.   When can she start?

(Maria takes Sophia by the hand.)

MARIA.   Come. I show you how.

CONSTANCE.   Right now?

MARIA.   Captain Almy right. Maria need
                          help. You want job too.

CONSTANCE.   No, I am a teacher. I do not desire
                          more work than that.

MARIA.   Then you go. Much sails to make
                          and not time enough. Husband
                          bastard off whaling! Leave me here
                          with his work and mine. Men no
                          damn good . . .'cept for one thing.

CONSTANCE.   Adam will pick you up, Sophia.
                          Thank you for your kindness,
                          Mrs.—

MARIA.   Maria! This not kindness; this
                          business.

CONSTANCE.   Yes, Maria. Thank you.

(She exits. As Maria goes to show Sophia the ropes, the
    LIGHTS COME DOWN SLOWLY.)

ACT I, SCENE VI

SCENE: LIGHTS   COMES   UP   on
                      CHARLES and THOMAS in
                      Clarke's office a few weeks later.
                      Thomas   is   going   through   an
                      account book while Charles sits
                      across from him. After a moment,
                      Thomas looks up and slaps the
                      book shut.

THOMAS.   So, young man, I think it is high
                      time we put you back to work.

CHARLES.   I have no objection to such a
                      course of action as that. I am ready.

THOMAS.   Well rested, are you?

CHARLES.   Yes sir.

THOMAS.   Yearning for your mistress?

CHARLES.   Sir?

THOMAS.   The sea?

CHARLES.   Of course—the sea.

THOMAS.   Did you think I was speaking of
                     something else?

CHARLES.   No sir, I was—yes, I suppose I did
                     for a moment.

THOMAS.   We are both men of the world,
                     Charles; I would not find it
                     unobjectionable if you were to seek
                     sanctuary in the company of
                     someone—

CHARLES.   I can assure you, Sir, that I have no
                     intention of finding comfort other
                     than with Constance from now to
                     perpetuity.

THOMAS.   That is a long time, Charles. (A
                     beat.) In any case, I can surmise
                     from such a statement of fact that
                     the—comfort--you find in my
                     daughter's arms is sufficient to
                     meet all of you needs, for
                     companionship and such.

CHARLES.   That would not be an inaccurate
                     assessment.

THOMAS.   Excellent! And I can tell from her
                     cheerful demeanor when you are
                     about that her needs are being
                     satisfied as well. (Opens a decanter

of liquor.) I think we should drink
to it.

(He pours and hands Charles a glass.)

THOMAS.   To—the fulfillment of our mutual
                   desires.

CHARLES.   Here. Here.

(They drink. Charles takes a gulp and then chokes.)

THOMAS.   Guinea rum, Son. Be careful.

CHARLES.   Powerful stuff.

THOMAS.   Which is why it is so desired in the
                   trade. (He pours Charles another.)
                   Now—down to business.

(Thomas crosses to a chart of the Atlantic Ocean on the
wall. He points to the chart as he continues.)

THOMAS.   Have you ever made a crossing,
                   Charles?

CHARLES.   No sir. But as you well know, I
                   have been sailing between the West
                   Indies and Charleston since I was
                   14 and between Newport and
                   Charleston for the past five years in
                   your employ.

THOMAS.   But you are not afraid of a run
                   across the Atlantic?

CHARLES.   I respect the sea, Sir; I do not fear
                   it.

THOMAS.   Good. It is my intention to involve
                  you more directly in my African
                  trade . . . if you have no objection,
                  of course.

CHARLES.   My only—reluctance would be that
                  my wedding would be delayed.

THOMAS.   I have taken that into
                  consideration, Charles. The date
                  you set is eight months away. That
                  gives you more than enough time
                  to complete this enterprise, and I
                  think it important that you
                  familiarize more intimately with
                  my—our—trade in Africa before
                  you join the family.

CHARLES.   Very well, Sir. What is the nature of
                  your trade in Africa?

THOMAS.   It is not just my trade, Charles; it is
                  an enterprise that involves well-
                  nigh all the mercantile families of
                  this city, if not the state. Let me
                  assure you that the investors, who
                  shall remained unnamed at this
                  point, are the cream of Newport
                  society and bear names you would
                  undoubtedly recognize.

CHARLES.   Why should the investors remain
                  unnamed?

THOMAS.   It is a common practice.

CHARLES.   But it has nothing to do with the
                nature of the trade?

THOMAS.   Have I made a statement that
                would lead you to believe that?

CHARLES.   Should I inquire further about the
                nature of your African trade?

THOMAS.   Rum! Guinea rum, much like what
                you are drinking presently is traded
                on the West African coast for a
                number of—products that may or
                may not find their way back to
                New England.

CHARLES.   Products such as . . .

THOMAS.   Palm oil, ivory, various African
                trinkets and tribal implements that
                are valued by collectors.

CHARLES.   So I would be returning to
                Newport or Boston from Africa.

THOMAS.   You know better than that, Charles.

CHARLES.   I know too then that I would be
                trading for more than African ivory
                and palm oil. Sir, you must
                understand that although I am
                from Charleston, my southern
                roots do not run nearly as deep as
                those of my brother.

THOMAS.   And what you must understand,
                Charles is that everything you see

out that window—that which belongs to me and that which belongs to the other mercantile families of Newport was built on this trade. And let me assure you that my future as well as yours depends to a large extent on this trade.

CHARLES. Constance knows nothing of this trade?

THOMAS. As I told you before, she must never know.

CHARLES. Surely there is another enterprise by which you can satisfy the growth expectations of your investors' capital.

THOMAS. And mine as well. But in answer to your question: there is no other trade that even approaches the profitability of the African trade. The South is planting more and more land in cotton; Northern states are passing post-nati manumission acts. The demand for labor is growing in the South along with the size of the fields planted in cotton. Prices are at an all-time high. We must take advantage of this market while it is there.

CHARLES. I do not know that I can do this, Sir.

THOMAS.   This is business, Charles. Nothing
                 more and nothing less. It is no
                 different than hauling lumber.

CHARLES.   It is a matter of trust; I do not wish
                 to deceive Constance.

THOMAS.   Charles, listen to me. I will not
                 accept a negative response from
                 you on this matter. The house I am
                 building for you and Constance is
                 being constructed on the African
                 trade. Constance's life of privilege
                 is built on that trade—

CHARLES.   But she is unaware of that!

THOMAS.   That is as it should be.

CHARLES.   What you are asking for me to do is
                 to dishonor her?

THOMAS.   Have you not already dishonored
                 her, Charles?

CHARLES.   Sir?

THOMAS.   Have I not turned a blind eye to
                 the intimacy that you and my
                 daughter have shared for some
                 time now?

CHARLES.   I was not aware that . . .

THOMAS.   I knew the nature of your
                 relationship with Constance? (A
                 beat) Why would I choose to
                 spend the night in an inn when I

62

knew you were calling on
Constance if I had not known you
were engaged in an intimate
relationship with my daughter?

CHARLES.   I know not.

THOMAS.   For freely giving my daughter to
              you, do you not feel in the least bit
              obliged to return this small favor?

CHARLES.   Ah . . . only now I see how
              business is conducted outside the
              theoretical realm of academia.

THOMAS.   You will not even command *The
              Rising Sun*; you will serve as First
              Mate, replacing one who has taken
              ill. On this voyage, I only desire
              that you learn the trade. On
              subsequent voyages, you will have
              command of your own ship.

CHARLES.   When do we sail?

THOMAS.   As soon as I acquire another 50
              hogshead rum for trading
              purposes—with 32 distilleries on
              this island, probably within the
              week. I will send my man, Adam,
              with you.

CHARLES.   Is he not working out in the
              stables?

THOMAS.   Adam is a fine worker; I hate to
              lose him, however I think you will

find him to be of more use to you
than he will be to me here.

CHARLES. He has in him a—rebellious streak.

THOMAS. It will be quelled before he
embarks.

CHARLES. Not with the whip.

THOMAS. I have never raised a hand to harm
one of my slaves.

CHARLES. I am gratified to hear it. (A beat.)
Have you ever lifted a finger to
truly help one?

THOMAS. Empty words coming from a
Southern gentleman, Charles.

CHARLES. Of course, you are right. I offer my
apology if I have offended you, Sir.

THOMAS. None taken.

CHARLES. Have you told Constance about
this?

THOMAS. It is not my place to bring her such
bad tidings.

CHARLES. You left that pleasure to me?

THOMAS. Yes, that among others.

CHARLES. Then I must be on my way, Sir.

THOMAS. God be with you.

CHARLES (exiting). As he is with you, Sir.

(BLACKOUT)

ACT I, SCENE VII

SCENE:

LIGHTS COME UP on SOPHIA, ADAM, CONSTANCE, and CHARLES later that afternoon. Constance is spreading a quilt on the ground on a cliff overlooking a wide expanse of the Atlantic ocean. Sophia and Adam are giving her a hand as Charles stands by holding a picnic basket. When the quilt is spread out and the corners anchored, Constance kneels down.

CONSTANCE.

Sweetheart, come sit here and hand me the basket. Sophia, you and Adam sit with us—there.

SOPHIA.

Ma'am?

CHARLES (not sure about this). Constance . . .

CONSTANCE.

Come now, sit, both of you.

ADAM. Massa Charles . . . ?

CONSTANCE. And I would prefer that neither of you use the term master ever again. Charles is not your master. Nor am I Sophia's. Do you understand that?

SOPHIA. Yes, Miss Constance.

CONSTANCE. And if you insist on calling me, Miss Constance, I shall call you Miss Sophia.

ADAM. What do I call—

CONSTANCE. Charles?

ADAM. Yes . . .

CONSTANCE. Call him what I call him.

ADAM. No, ma'am! Ain't calling him "Sweetheart."

CHARLES. Call me—Mr. Charles. And I will call you—Mr. Adam? How does that suit you?

ADAM. "Mr. Adam." I likes that. I likes that jist fine. "Mr. Adam."

CONSTANCE. Mr. Adam, won't you and your lady join us here on the quilt for a bite to eat?

(They're not sure about this; this is crossing a new boundary. After a moment, Adam takes Sophia's hand and they step onto the quilt.)

ADAM.   Thank you, Miss Constance, I think
                   we would like to very much to join
                   you for a bite—if Mr. Charles has
                   no objection.

CHARLES.   No, Mr. Adam, I have no
                   objection. Please—join us.

CONSTANCE.   Is this not just grand—thank you
                   God, for this one blissful moment
                   in this beautiful place with these
                   good people.

ADAM.   Amen to that.

CONSTANCE.   Charles, did I tell you that Sophia is
                   teaching Adam to read?

CHARLES (not sure this is a good thing). Is that so?

ADAM.   Yes sir. I can reads entire
                   paragraphs without stopping.

SOPHIA.   He learn quick, Mr. Charles. Won't
                   be long 'fore he readin' whole
                   books.

ADAM.   My mind thirsty for words and
                   ideas same as my body is for water
                   come plantin' time. I findin' ideas
                   grow jist like a cotton plant—
                   shootin' right up through the earth.

CHARLES. Which is exactly why you were not taught to read in Virginia.

CONSTANCE. Charles, why don't you ask Mr. Adam to read for us?

CHARLES. Of course. Mr. Adam . . .

ADAM. Yes, Mr. Charles.

CHARLES. Would you be kind enough to favor these ladies and me with a recitation?

ADAM. I don't know about that, but I would be most happily to reads to you from a book.

CHARLES. Please.

(Constance hands Adam a book.)

ADAM (reading). We—we holds—

SOPHIA. Hold.

ADAM. We hold these truths to be self—evident.

SOPHIA. Very good.

CHARLES. Constance . . .

CONSTANCE. Just listen.

ADAM. . . . that all men are created equal, that they are—en—dow—ed—endowed by—by—God—with certain un—alienable—Rights, that among these are Life, Liberty and the pursuit of Happiness.

(Sophia kisses him on the cheek.)

CONSTANCE.   That was jist fine, Mr. Adam! Just fine.

CHARLES.   You read very well, Mr. Adam. Very well indeed.

ADAM.   You knows, Mr. Charles, sometimes I can read the words if I sounds them out, but then I don't know zakly what they means.

CHARLES.   Sometime I don't know either.

ADAM.   What *these* words mean, Mr. Charles?

CHARLES (after a moment). What those words mean, what they *really* mean, is that if you want to know what is truly in a man's heart, you must look at what he does rather than at what he says or writes in a document.

ADAM.   Jist as I thought.

CHARLES.   I am very sorry.

ADAM.   Wished everybody was.

SOPHIA.   Well, jist look at all that ocean out there.

ADAM.

How far across is it, Miss Constance?

CONSTANCE.

Charles knows more of the sea than do I. How far is it across, Charles?

CHARLES.

Depends on where you want to go. Great Britain is about 2,000 miles; your homeland is 1,000 miles further.

ADAM.

Virginia my homeland.

CHARLES.

Please accept my apology. The West Coast of Africa is approximately 3,000 miles from here.

SOPHIA.

There talk of sending freed slaves back to Africa. That right, Mr. Charles?

ADAM.

Neither of us ever been in Africa. I born in Virginia, Sophia in South Carolina. What we have to return to in Africa?

CHARLES.

I—don't know.

CONSTANCE.

There *is* talk of sending freed slaves back to Africa. Even the abolitionists speak of it.

ADAM.

If we be free, why not we be free to stay here?

CHARLES.

Because we do not have any idea of what to do with you. Neither the abolitionists, nor the government, nor the slaveholders have any idea of where freed Negroes will fit into our white society. That is the truth of the matter. But you need not worry about being sent to Africa. If there is no money to be made in sending you back, you will remain in this country.

ADAM. That be good. When I free—I wants to find my own happiness and life and liberty.

CHARLES. So do we all.

CONSTANCE. Charles, are you not finding your happiness in what you're doing? (Silence.) Charles?

CHARLES. I have a business obligation to fulfill, Constance, one that will take me away from you for a while.

CONSTANCE. You are going away?

CHARLES. Yes.

CONSTANCE. When?

CHARLES. Soon. Probably within the week.

(Sophia stands and pulls Adam up.)

SOPHIA. We must go. Thank you, Miss Constance, Mr. Charles.

(They exit.)

CONSTANCE.   Charles, where are you going?

CHARLES.   Africa.

CONSTANCE.   Africa?

CHARLES.   Yes. I need to learn the African trade.

CONSTANCE.   You have never been before.

CHARLES.   That is why I am going.

CONSTANCE.   Father is sending you?

CHARLES.   It is my job, Constance. It is the life I—we have chosen. We knew there would be separations.

CONSTANCE.   What about our wedding?

CHARLES.   If all goes well, I'll be back in seven months—nothing will have to change.

CONSTANCE.   Have you *ever* been on a sea voyage when everything went well?

CHARLES.   Admittedly, there are uncertainties that cannot be predicted.

CONSTANCE.   The fever! Small pox! Storms! I might never see you again.

CHARLES.   I will return to you, Constance. We will marry as soon as I get home, whenever that is.

CONSTANCE.   You told me you were only going
              to be involved in the coastal trade.

CHARLES.   I know that, but . . . circumstances
              dictate that I make this voyage.

CONSTANCE.   What circumstances?

CHARLES.   The First Mate on *The Rising Sun*
              has fallen ill; your father has asked
              me to take his place.

CONSTANCE.   And you said you would?

CHARLES.   Constance, I—owe your father my
              allegiance.

CONSTANCE.   Do you not owe your allegiance to
              me as well?

CHARLES.   Of course, I do, but it is through
              my allegiance to your father that I
              can make myself worthy enough to
              even offer myself to you.

CONSTANCE.   I expect nothing more from you
              than your love, Charles. I can
              manage quite well without the
              finery that money provides if I am
              loved.

CHARLES.   But my love for you requires me to
              offer you much more.

CONSTANCE.   So—to give me more than I even
              desire, you will abandon me for as
              long as seven months, a year
              perhaps?

CHARLES.   Abandon is a strong word,
                Constance.

CONSTANCE.   Is love not a stronger one?

CHARLES.   Constance . . . my love for you
                exceeds all else on this planet. You
                must know and believe that.

CONSTANCE.   What I know is that to truly know
                what is in a man's heart, you must
                look at what he does, rather than
                what he says.

CHARLES.   Constance . . .

CONSTANCE.   Is that not what you told Adam?

CHARLES.   It is a bad omen to depart on such
                an ill wind.

CONSTANCE.   Then I beg you not go.

CHARLES.   Constance, I must go—for reasons
                that are inexplicable and at the
                same time compelling. Forgive me.

CONSTANCE.   It is for God to forgive, Charles.
                He brought us together, and it is
                you who chooses to break us apart.
                For that, I cannot forgive you.

CHARLES.   I shall come back to you,
                Constance. You have my word.

CONSTANCE.   Fare thee well then Charles. I wish
                you a fair wind and following seas.

(Constance gathers up the quilt and walks away
as the LIGHT COME DOWN TO END ACT I.)

A LITTLE LOWER THAN THE ANGELS

by

David W. Christner

ACT II, SCENE I

SCENE:	LIGHTS COME UP on MARIA and SOPHIA in the sail-loft. Both are sewing at separate ends of a large white sail.
MARIA.	Sophia, you good worker, learn fast. I make you into good sail maker.
SOPHIA.	Same as making dress, only bigger.
MARIA.	Much bigger—less you got giant womens in the South.
SOPHIA.	No, not this big. Some got big *heads* though.
MARIA.	You like it here, okay?
SOPHIA.	In Newport?
MARIA.	My shop? You like being maker of sails?

SOPHIA.	I like it fine; first time I ever paid for working. I feel rich already.
MARIA.	You keep working good, I give you more money.
SOPHIA.	More money?
MARIA.	I no slave master.
SOPHIA.	How much more?
MARIA.	Jist more. What you need money for anyway? Miss Constance, Mr. Clarke not take good care of you— give you roof overhead, plenty to eat?
SOPHIA.	When I free, I got to make my own way though. Need money for family too.
MARIA.	What family you got?
SOPHIA.	Maybe I got family in Charleston still. Wants to make them free too.
MARIA.	What 'bout, Mr. Adam?
SOPHIA.	What 'bout him?
MARIA.	Don't know.
SOPHIA.	Then you tend your sail; I tend mine. Mr. Adam my business.
MARIA.	Think he a little sweet on you?

SOPHIA.   Never mind what I thinks.

MARIA.   Maybe Sophia little sweet on him?

SOPHIA.   Maybe so. Don't matter now
                 anyway; he gone. Went off with
                 Mr. Charles on *Rising Sun.*

MARIA.   *Rising Sun?* He go on that devil
                 ship?

SOPHIA.   That right. What wrong with that?

MARIA.   *Rising Sun* a slaver, bound for
                 Africa.

SOPHIA.   No! Mr. Charles on board; he no
                 take Africans for slaves; he be
                 freein' Sophia.

MARIA.   You know what you know; I know
                 what I know.

SOPHIA.   Mr. Charles . . . he *never* take Adam
                 with him on slaver; Adam . . .

CONSTANCE (off). Mrs. Pires . . . Mrs. Pires.

MARIA.   Maria! Come in.

(CONSTANCE enters.)

CONSTANCE.   Please excuse this intrusion, but—I
                 have news for Sophia that just
                 could not wait.

MARIA.   You tell her news if she keep
                 working.

79

CONSTANCE.   Thank you.

MARIA.   I have to keep working too, many sails to make, not time enough. Husband gone off whaling—leave all work to me. Men no damn good—'cept for one thing.

CONSTANCE.   Yes, you mentioned that. I'm sorry.

MARIA.   So . . . what news you got?

CONSTANCE.   It is for Sophia.

MARIA.   Know who! Want to know what.

CONSTANCE (takes out paper). Sophia, you are free; before Charles left, he set you free. I have the papers.

MARIA.   You free to stay right there and make sails; that how free you are.

SOPHIA.   Free?

CONSTANCE.   As a bird.

MARIA.   Jailbird maybe.

CONSTANCE.   Is it not wonderful?

SOPHIA.   Don't know. Don't know how I supposed to feel to be free.

CONSTANCE.   I had no doubt that he would set you free eventually, but—

SOPHIA.   Maybe he jist did it so you be less
                        angry with him for going.

CONSTANCE.   I do not care; the important thing is
                        that he did it!

SOPHIA.   So now, all the money I make is for
                        me?

CONSTANCE.   Yes, of course.

SOPHIA.   And I can spend it however I want.

CONSTANCE.   We'll be happy to provide you with
                        some guidance on—investing it, to
                        make it grow.

MARIA.   Oh yeah, invest in *Rising Sun*; make
                        much monies.

CONSTANCE.   *Rising Sun?*

SOPHIA.   I jist tell her Adam and Mr. Charles
                        ship out for Africa.

(Sophia turns away.)

CONSTANCE.   Sophia . . . is something wrong?

SOPHIA.   Tell Miss Constance what you told
                        me.

MARIA.   Don't pay me no mind; I jist hear
                        things.

CONSTANCE.   What—kinds of things?

MARIA.

Don't bother yourself with what I hear, Miss Constance. I will give Sophia the rest of the day off; she should get to enjoy her freedom on this one day. You two go now; I finish up here.

SOPHIA.

No, you gots to tell her; if it be true—maybe she can do something to stop it.

CONSTANCE.

Mrs. Pires . . .

MARIA.

Rising Sun in African trade; that all I know.

CONSTANCE.

That is true; she is taking rum to trade for palm oil and ivory.

MARIA.

Who tell you that?

CONSTANCE.

My father.

MARIA.

What need palm oil and ivory for? Got more than enough whale oil and ivory in New Bedford and Nantucket. Much closer. African trade not for those things.

CONSTANCE.

What are you saying, Mrs. Pires?

MARIA.

I say you go to shipping office— look at manifest of *Rising Sun* to find out about African trade. That all I'm sayin'.

CONSTANCE.

Very well, I shall do just that. Miss Sophia . . .

SOPHIA.   I gots to work, Miss Constance.
                  Now that I free, I gots to work
                  even harder.

CONSTANCE.   Very well. I will see you at home
                  this evening.

SOPHIA.   Yes ma'am.

CONSTANCE.   Yes what?

SOPHIA.   Miss Constance.

CONSTANCE.   All right. I will see you at home this
                  evening, Miss Sophia. (A beat.)
                  Good day, Mrs. Pires.

MARIA.   Maria!

(LIGHTS COME DOWN SLOWLY.)

ACT II, SCENE II

SCENE: LIGHTS COME UP on THOMAS
                        in his office overlooking the wharf
                        later the same day. He is working at
                        his   desk   when   CONTANCE
                        ENTERS unannounced. He closes
                        an account book and gets up.

THOMAS.   Constance, what an unexpected
                        pleasure.

CONSTANCE.   Perhaps not, Father.

THOMAS.   Did you tell Sophia her good news?

CONSTANCE.   Yes, I did. I just came from there.
                        And while I was delivering Sophia's
                        good news, I fear I may have come
                        upon some bad.

THOMAS.   Is that so?

CONSTANCE.   Father, I'll get right to the point.

THOMAS.   You ordinarily do.

CONSTANCE.   What exactly is the nature of your
                 African trade?

THOMAS.   Rum. Guinea rum they call it—
                 distilled right here on the island.
                 Most of it in Newport. You can
                 find plenty of it in any alehouse.

CONSTANCE.   I prefer not to frequent the
                 alehouses, Father.

THOMAS.   Of course not. The rum that is not
                 consumed locally is exported.

CONSTANCE.   I know what you export; what I
                 want to know is—what you import.

THOMAS.   Various items that can be made to
                 be of use to someone else—palm
                 oil, ivory, African implements and
                 art objects for collectors. Many
                 things.

CONSTANCE.   But are your ships not routed
                 through the West Indies on their
                 voyage home.

THOMAS.   This is no secret about it; that is
                 where I buy sugar and molasses for
                 the local distilleries to make rum.

CONSTANCE.   May I see the manifest for this
                 voyage of the *Rising Sun*?

THOMAS.   It wouldn't make any sense to
                 you—

CONSTANCE.   Is it not written in English?

THOMAS.   What I mean—is that everything
               that goes on the ship would not
               necessarily have meaning to you, or
               that the presence of some items are
               likely to be misinterpreted.

CONSTANCE.   Does that mean I cannot see the
               manifest?

THOMAS.   I don't see how seeing the manifest
               would prove to be of any practical
               value.

CONSTANCE.   Father, look me in the eye and
               swear to me on your honor as a
               gentleman that you did not send
               Charles on a slaver.

THOMAS.   Constance, you have since birth,
               reaped the rewards of my business
               affairs without knowledge of what
               exactly they involved. I see no
               reason for that to change.

CONSTANCE.   Then it is true?

THOMAS.   Believe what you will. But know
               too that our life—your life—has
               been built on that trade. And this
               family is not the only prominent
               family on this island nor in this
               state to reap the reward of the
               African trade.

CONSTANCE. It is incomprehensible and inexcusable to me that you would involve Charles in this sordid business.

THOMAS. You will both get used to the comforts it provides. Indeed, you already are.

CONSTANCE (thinks, then). No. No! I can live without such comforts. I can live without status. I can even live without love if it has to come to that. But I cannot live without honor. And I see that I was mistaken to think that that was the case with you.

THOMAS (as Constance exits). Constance . . . wait. (She stops.) Where are you going?

CONSTANCE. To find other accommodations for Miss Sophia and me.

THOMAS. Your house is finished; you can go there.

CONSTANCE. No. It is tainted. We'll go elsewhere.

THOMAS. You are being ridiculous.

CONSTANCE. Have I not always taken that path in your eyes?

THOMAS. Constance, women need not concern themselves with these matters. Profit cannot be made on conscience; it is made on a good business sense.

CONSTANCE.   Goodbye, Father.

THOMAS.   Constance! (She keeps going.) Charles will set you straight when he returns. Until then I want you in that house!

(LIGHTS COME DOWN as Constance turns and storms out.)

ACT II, SCENE III

SCENE:

LIGHTS COME UP on CHARLES and ADAM a week or so later on the after deck of the sloop *rising sun*. Charles has the watch; Adam is at the helm. It is night; stars shine overhead, and in the moonless night, the scene is lighted in an eerie blue light.

ADAM.

Still headin' east, Mr. Charles.

CHARLES.

What makes you think that?

ADAM.

Sun rise in the east, Mr. Charles. Set in the west. Not hard to figure out which we goin'.

CHARLES.

We are heading east. East-southeast.

ADAM (after a moment). West Indies pretty much due south of Newport, Mr. Charles? That not right?

CHARLES. That is correct, Mr. Adam.

ADAM. So . . . where we be goin', headin' east like this?

CHARLES. Africa.

ADAM. Africa?

CHARLES. I think you were aware of it.

ADAM. I figured it; I saw them chains and such below. But I not *knowed* it until now.

CHARLES. I am very sorry it has come to this.

ADAM. We all sorry, Mr. Charles. For one thing or another.

CHARLES. This is not what I would have chosen to do; this is, in fact, the very thing I wanted to avoid doing.

ADAM. We all gots to make choices every day, Mr. Charles. Course you gots to make a lot more of them than I do—cause you makin' most of my choices for me. Relieves me of that burden; yes it does.

CHARLES. Sometimes, however, it *appears* as if you have no choice at all.

ADAM.   Oh, I know what you means there
                 all right.

CHARLES.   Constance's father put me in a very
                 difficult position, a position in
                 which I had to make a choice I did
                 not wish to make.

ADAM.   Did same thing to me! Said to me:
                 "Adam, I sending you on a voyage
                 with Mr. Charles. You look after
                 him," he says. "And when he gets
                 back home, I make you a free
                 man."

CHARLES.   He didn't tell you anything about—
                 the voyage? Where we were going?
                 What we would be trading for?

ADAM.   No, but I knowed what was about
                 though. Everyone know he runs
                 slavers to Africa, so I know he
                 asking me to help you make slaves
                 of black people—steal them from
                 homes and take them across the sea
                 to sell. I no want to be no part of it,
                 but Mr. Clarke know I loves
                 Sophia, know I want to marry her;
                 so if I free and she free, then we
                 can marry. So he know I do what
                 he say. What choice I got, Mr.
                 Adam, but to make you my new
                 best friend?

CHARLES.   That is very much like the choice
                 he gave me.

ADAM.   But you and Miss Constance already be free.

CHARLES.   Yes . . . maybe *too* free.

ADAM   Oh . . . that Mr. Clarke, he sure know how to get what he want.

CHARLES.   He does indeed. (A beat.) So . . . new best friend, I vow to get you back safe to your Sophia.

ADAM.   And I will get you back to Miss Constance. We be like brothers now.

CHARLES.   Yes, like brothers and *all* you have to do is get me back; you will not have to help—in this other business.

ADAM.   I hope that be true; I most surely do. It break my heart to hurt my other brothers.

CHARLES (looks up). Starting to blow—may have to shorten sail.

ADAM.   Whatever you say, Mr. Charles.

(LIGHTS COME DOWN SLOWLY.)

ACT II, SCENE IV

SCENE:

LIGHTS COME UP on SOPHIA and CONSTANCE in a small bedroom a few days later. Constance is seated at a dressing table, writing a letter; Sophia is changing for bed and washing up from a pan and pitcher of water on a dresser.

CONSTANCE.

I don't know exactly how the mail system works, Sophia. It's a little like putting a message in a bottle, but correspondence does by the grace of God somehow get through. In any case, it takes weeks for letters to be exchanged in either direction.

SOPHIA.

You still angry with Mr. Charles, Miss Constance?

CONSTANCE.	No, I cannot remain long angry at Charles. He has a good heart, and in my heart I know that he will do what is right.
SOPHIA.	How will he know?
CONSTANCE.	Everyone knows what is right.
SOPHIA.	Then why so many choose to do wrong?
CONSTANCE.	I don't know, Sophia. Maybe it is our nature. Certainly it is not what God planned for us. In any case, I cannot seem to stop loving Charles, no matter how angry I get at him.
SOPHIA.	Hard to stay mad at man you love; love make you blind to faults.
CONSTANCE.	Sophia, do you feel that way about Adam?
SOPHIA.	Yes, I do, but . . . I don't know that I got a right to be feelin' that way or not.
CONSTANCE.	Love is God's greatest gift. It is perfectly natural to fall in love, Sophia.
SOPHIA.	I know that, but Adam a good man, a trusting man, and he not even want to—take me 'fore we're married. But . . . maybe I not be good enough for him.

CONSTANCE.   Of course you are!

SOPHIA.   You don't understand, Miss Constance—I—spoilt.

CONSTANCE.   Spoiled?

SOPHIA.   That right.

CONSTANCE.   You have—been with a man?

SOPHIA.   Yes, Miss Sophia. I even has a baby—almost five years old now.

CONSTANCE.   Five? You must have been a child yourself . . . where is this child?

SOPHIA.   Charleston. That's why I got to get some monies; I want to buy my son out of slavery to have him with me and Adam. But don't know if Adam want us.

CONSTANCE.   Where is the father?

SOPHIA.   He gone!

CONSTANCE.   Gone? Where?

SOPHIA.   Jist gone. Don't know where to.

CONSTANCE.   He was sold?

SOPHIA.   Don't know . . . but he gone.

CONSTANCE.   Mr. Adam doesn't know about this?

SOPHIA.   I not know how to tell him; afraid he leave me.

CONSTANCE.   He won't leave you, Miss Sophia. He will not. But you must write him; you must tell him. I will write Charles; I will tell him to pick up your son in Charleston; no matter what he has to pay. We will get him for you. I promise you that.

SOPHIA.   Thank you, Miss Constance. You truly kind to me, and I have nothing to give you in return.

CONSTANCE.   You give me your friendship, Miss Sophia. That is enough.

SOPHIA.   I wish I had more to give.

CONSTANCE.   Maybe . . . you can—give me some . . . information. (A few beats.) Is it true that Maria Pires is a midwife?

SOPHIA.   She say so. But—I don't need midwife; me and Adam never—

CONSTANCE.   Not for you.

SOPHIA.   Oh . . .

CONSTANCE.   Tell me, Sophia, when . . . before you had your child . . . how long before did you know that you were—carrying a child? How soon did you know after—you had relations?

SOPHIA.

I think I know almost immediately—like a day or two after. I felt—different inside. Then the blood didn't come, and my bosom was tender. I knew for sure then, but even 'fore that, I knew I was changed.

CONSTANCE.

Did you feel—any sickness?

SOPHIA.

Every morning! Yes, I did. Sick every mornin' for some time.

CONSTANCE.

Oh God!

SOPHIA.

Miss Constance . . . you not . . .

CONSTANCE.

I'm afraid I am.

SOPHIA.

You need see doctor to be sure.

CONSTANCE.

Did you see a doctor?

SOPHIA.

No. Midwife. But you . . . white.

CONSTANCE.

This must be our secret, Sophia.

SOPHIA.

Miss Constance, Mr. Charles not comin' home for seven maybe eight months. People gonna know. No secret for very long.

CONSTANCE.

Still, I don't want you to tell anyone yet. I—have to think.

SOPHIA.

You *way* past the point of thinkin', Miss Constance. You best write Mr.

Charles and tell' em to get back
here for a wedding.

CONSTANCE.   No! Charles mustn't know.

SOPHIA.   He gots to know!

CONSTANCE.   No! He must do what he has to do
                    without knowing about me.

SOPHIA.   But Miss Constance, he
                    responsible.

CONSTANCE.   Not any more so than am I. (Starts
                    to break.) Promise me you will not
                    tell him. Or Adam. Promise!

SOPHIA.   If that what you want.

CONSTANCE (breaking). It is. (A few beats.) Oh, god,
                    Sophia, what have I done?

(They embrace.)

SOPHIA.   You just done what people in love
                    do; nothin' wrong in that. Don't be
                    'fraid, Miss Constance. Miss Sophia
                    here to take care of you.

(Constance begins to weep as the
LIGHTS DOWN TO END THE SCENE.)

ACT II, SCENE V

SCENE:

LIGHTS COME UP on ADAM on the after deck of a sloop. The sloop is anchored off the Guinea coast of Africa. He is reading a letter. A LIGHT COMES UP on SOPHIA.

SOPHIA.

My Dear Man,

Hope you doing fine on this voyage. By now I know you on a slaver bound for Africa, and I not too happy 'bout that. Probably not nearly so unhappy as you are though. I know how you must hates it; hates the men making you do what you have to do to your own kind. But you gots to do it, just this one time. You gots to do it for me and for you and for Miss Constance.

She say Mr. Charles do the right thing; I don't know what that be; maybe he don't know either, but he gonna know. Miss Constance say so; she tell him 'bout Charlotte Amalie. That free port now; no

more tradin' slaves there; King of
Denmark say so. Quakers there to
send slaves back to Africa 'fore
they git sold. Moses sending slaves
home; jist like in the Bible, but
Moses Brown from Providence do
it this time, deliver the people from
slavery.

Adam, I wants you to come home
to me. Mr. Charles done make me a
free woman; I free right now; free
as a bird. Working harder than ever
now though. Being free no picnic.
Gots to get monies to buy
someone—my—son in Charleston.
That right. I got a son. I tell you all
'bout it when you come home.
Should of told you sooner, but
didn't know how. Sorry for that.
Anyway, he live with us when we
married. That why you got to come
home; don't be doin' somethin'
stupid gonna git you in trouble.
You swallow your pride if you
havta for a little longer. When you
git home, you be free to. Then we
can be family; be Yankees and build
a life away from what we had down
there. I already a plenty good sail-
maker. Just miss you that's all.

I missin' you most terribly. I wants
to take you to my bed as my
husband and not let you go. You
hear Adam. I wants you home. And
you gots to know I love you no

matter what happens or has happened. If you was to have had a girl in Virginia, that okay. That before you know me.

Oil burnin' down now, so I gots to go. Busy day tomorrow. Much sails to make and not time enough.

Love you, Adam. Loves you with everything I got.

Your Sophia.

(Adam smiles, shakes his head, maybe wipes away a tear, folds the letter and slips it in his pocket as CHARLES enters from "below."

CHARLES.	All is quiet.
ADAM.	You sure, Mr. Charles? Could of swore I heard some weeping comin' from down there.
CHARLES.	All is *secure*.
ADAM.	Yes sir, I understands now—all chains holdin' fast. Ain't no hint or chance of rebellion. All them Africans tied down real good.
CHARLES.	Readin' Sophia's letter again.
ADAM.	That right. Got the whole thing memorized by now.
CHARLES.	We will be leaving in a few days; we send mail back on the Avenger,

which is Boston bound. If you
want to write Sophia—

ADAM.　　　　Would you help me, Mr. Charles? I
reads pretty good, but I needs a lots
of work with my writin'.

CHARLES.　　　Of course, I'll help you Mr. Adam.
Give me a moment to find paper
and a writing instrument.

(He starts "below.")

ADAM.　　　　Wouldn't hurt to have some
Guinea rum too, Mr. Charles. No
sir, wouldn't hurt none at all.

CHARLES (exiting). If we have not yet traded it all, I will
see what I can do.

ADAM (composing aloud). Dear Miss Sophia—Dear
Sophia—Sophia Dear?

(Charles returns with paper, pen, ink, a bottle of rum and
two mugs.)

ADAM.　　　　Now, we can gits down to business.

CHARLES.　　　First a drink.

ADAM.　　　　That *is* the business.

(Charles pours and passes a mug to Adam. Then he finds a
place to sit to compose Adam's letter.)

CHARLES.　　　You tell me what to write, and I
will write it.

ADAM.   'Zakly like I tells you.

CHARLES.   You have my word.

ADAM.   Dear . . .

CHARLES.   Sophia.

ADAM.   *Miss* Sophia.

CHARLES.   Dear Miss Sophia.

(Charles drinks the rum as Adam composes and Charles writes.)

ADAM.   Mr. Charles and me is makin' out
                         jist fine here in Africa. We 'bout
                         got us a boatload of Africans, and
                         we be gittin' underway soon for
                         Havana in the West Indies to sell
                         'em. That right. Me and Mr.
                         Charles, slave traders now. Mr.
                         Charles, Captain of slave ship, and
                         I be his best boy. Mr. Charles
                         Captain now 'cause other captain
                         went and got hisself drowned in the
                         river. Saw it with my own eyes.

                         We was in the small boat, bringin'
                         back some Africans we traded
                         some Guinea rum for, and where
                         the mouth of the river runs into the
                         sea, it gits plenty rough and captain
                         fall right in without no help from
                         anybody. Now Adam's thinkin'
                         maybe I ought to do somethin' fore
                         he get pulled under by the current,

but then I decides that God must
of planned foe captain to fall in.
And if God planned foe captain to
fall in, Adam got no authority to
mess up God's plan, so me and
those other Africans, we just watch
him go away. Pulled further and
further away until we couldn't see
him no more. Then he be gone.
Gone to the fishes I thinks. I come
back and tell Mr. Charles he be
captain. God's will. That how Mr.
Charles become captain of a slaver.
Up to him to git us to West Indies
now. He in charge; what happens
to all of us now in *his* hands. Me
and all these Africans dependin' on
him.

Also, I gots to tell you. I ain't never
had no girl 'fore you. You Adam's
first love, and my only love. First
time I seen you I knew you the girl
for Adam; you make my heart beat
mighty fast; still I respect you. That
why I not want to take you till we
be man and wife. I want you plenty
bad now though. Gittin' damn tired
of lookin' at Mr. Charles all the
time. Boat too small a place for this
many peoples.

We sposed to go to Havana, but I
done told Mr. Charles 'bout
Charlotte Amalie, don't think he
knowed 'bout it, unlessin' Miss
Constance told him. And I don't

know 'bout that cause Mr. Charles
don't care to share her letters with
Adam. I gots to show him your
letters to make sure I'm reading 'em
right.

I gots to go now, Miss Sophia.
Gots some rum to drink 'fore it
vaporate in this African heat—or
until someone else (looks at
Charles) drinks it. Anyway, you wait
right there for me. I be back as
soon as Mr. Charles git me there.
I'm missin' you somethin' terrible,
and I loves you more than I know
how to say it. You jist wait. I be
there soon.

Your man,

Adam

Give my regards to Miss
Constance, and tell her I'm taking
care of Mr. Charles jist fine.

CHARLES.   That's a fine letter, Mr. Adam.

ADAM.   Can I sees it, Mr. Charles?

CHARLES (hands him the letter). Mr. Adam . . . if I had
                fallen in the river, would you have
                tried to pull *me* out?

ADAM.   Have to. We best friends. That not
                so?

CHARLES.   I mean, if you weren't under this—
                         obligation to get me home?

ADAM.   Oh . . . I sees what you means. (A
                         few beats.) I guess I have to figure
                         then if I coulds git back to Miss
                         Sophia by myself.

(Charles nods. There is a moment of silence that is
shattered when a CRY IS HEARD FROM BELOW. They
continue to sit in silence and drink rum. The CRIES
continue periodically.)

CHARLES.   Mr. Adam, do you think it is God's
                         plan that those Africans below
                         should be made into slaves?

ADAM.   Don't matter what I thinks, Mr.
                         Charles. What you think?

CHARLES.   I force myself not to think about it.

ADAM.   Miss Sophia tell me you do the
                         right thing; she say you man with
                         honor, not only wear face of honor
                         like other white mens who has
                         slaves.

CHARLES (distantly). No, I have no honor left; I
                         relinquished it the first time I stood
                         by and watched my brother beat a
                         slave in a cotton field. I fled my
                         home because I had not honor
                         enough to stand up for what is
                         right, and now . . . look at me . . .
                         (Adam looks away.) Look at me!
                         (Adam stares at him with fire in his

eyes. Another CRY COMES FROM BELOW.) When I see your back, I cannot help but wonder how many of those scars I put there. (A beat.) I know you hate me, Adam . . . and I can find no fault in your doing so.

ADAM.

That the rum talkin', Mr. Charles.

CHARLES.

Rum or not—it is God's truth. (A beat.) And you—all of you have no reason not to hate me—us—all of us. We say you are an inferior race, knowing all the while it is not so. God made us all equal; it is only by virtue of our power that we make and keep you unequal. We deny you education; we feed you only that which we won't eat; we house you in shacks and work you like beasts of the field until you have neither the energy nor the will to rebel. We deny you the opportunity to be equal, and then tell ourselves that you could not survive without us, when, in fact, we could not survive without you. (A few beats.) You could kill me, Adam. There are nearly 100 of you onboard and six of us. You could take over this ship at any time.

ADAM.

You right 'bout that.

CHARLES.

Why don't you?

ADAM.   Not God's plan.

CHARLES.   What is?

ADAM.   Don't know. I gots no more idea of
                   God's plan than does you.

(LIGHTS COME DOWN SLOWLY
TO END THE SCENE.)

ACT II, SCENE VI

SCENE: LIGHTS COMES UP on
                    CONSTANCE a few weeks later in
                    the small room she shares with
                    Sophia. She is standing at a mirror,
                    trying to see how much her
                    pregnancy is showing. She is
                    something like five months
                    pregnant now, and it shows. After a
                    moment, SOPHIA ENTERS.

CONSTANCE.   Oh, Sophia, I'm glad you have
                    returned.

SOPHIA.   Constance, someone here to see
                    you.

(They have become close friends and have dropped the
"Miss" when addressing one another.)

CONSTANCE.   Here? Who is it?

(THOMAS enters. Constance attempts to hide her
abdomen.)

CONSTANCE.   Father!

THOMAS.   Hello, Constance.

CONSTANCE.   Sophia! What is going on?

THOMAS.   I've come to take you home.

CONSTANCE.   Thank you, but my home is presently in this sail loft with Sophia.

THOMAS.   You both—occupy this single room?

CONSTANCE.   Mrs. Pires has been kind enough to let it to us at a very reasonable rate until we can find more suitable accommodations. We are really quite comfortable.

THOMAS.   Constance, nobody in this city is going to let you accommodations under the—circumstances.

CONSTANCE.   What—circumstances?

THOMAS.   You know very well what circumstances.

CONSTANCE.   Sophia?

SOPHIA.   I had to tell him, Constance; you not doing so good. Need to see real doctor.

CONSTANCE.   You promised!

SOPHIA.   You do the same if I sick, Constance. I know you would. I don't care where we live, but you need to see doctor. Listen to father now. He talkin' good sense.

CONSTANCE. I'm not sick! I'm simply—

THOMAS. Carrying a child—my grandchild, and I want to see that you have the best care available on this island. Constance, you must come home.

CONSTANCE. We will find our own home, Father.

THOMAS. Not in this town, you won't. (A beat.) Constance, you are with child; you are unmarried; you are living with—a Negro, a former slave. Who is going to have a place for you?

SOPHIA. He right, Constance. I try find us place all over this town; nobody else have place for us.

CONSTANCE. Did you go to the Quaker Meeting?

SOPHIA. They not let me in. I free to be outside, but not inside. But they tell Friends inside we need place to stay, but nobody have a place for us. Same thing at other churches.

THOMAS. I have a place for you—both of you.

CONSTANCE. Father, when will Charles be home?

THOMAS. Not soon enough to prevent a scandal. (A beat.) Had I known

about this—I never would have
sent him away.

CONSTANCE.   Really?

THOMAS.   Of course. I wouldn't have—
allowed you to be put in this
position.

CONSTANCE.   Not even to protect your
investment.

THOMAS.   Constance, please . . .

CONSTANCE.   Please what, Father?

THOMAS.   Don't hold me to such a high
standard.

CONSTANCE.   I did not set the standard; it was set
by the church and the framers of
the Constitution.

THOMAS.   I am not the only man in this city
that professes to occupy the moral
high ground, but, who, as a matter
of self-preservation, has to conduct
business on a lower level.

CONSTANCE.   I am well aware of that, Father, but
then I do not carry the name of any
of those other merchants or
investors. I carry your name.

THOMAS.   Constance, what must I do to bring
you home?

CONSTANCE.   You know very well what you must
              do.

(He shakes his head as Constance goes to Sophia and puts
an arm around her.)

CONSTANCE.   Can you not make a profit by
              trading something other than
              God's children?

THOMAS.   Constance, how can you condemn
              me for trading slaves? The
              abolitionists only desire to free
              them to sooth their moral outrage;
              they care nothing for these Negroes
              as human beings.

CONSTANCE.   These things take time, Father.

THOMAS.   No, Constance, they take strength
              and will, which you have in excess;
              God only know where you got it,
              certainly not from me. You have
              the strength to treat Sophia as a
              sister, to treat her as your moral
              and social equal. Few others are
              willing to take such a risk.

CONSTANCE.   It is not so hard to discern right
              from wrong, Father.

THOMAS.   Not to discern it, only to practice it.
              Come home, Constance—both of
              you.

CONSTANCE.   Will you give up the slave trade if
              we come home?

THOMAS.   Constance, it is a tangled web of
                 commerce and politics that I find
                 myself caught up in.

CONSTANCE.   That is my condition.

THOMAS.   So be it. I know your position is
                 morally right; even so, I cannot—
                 and I am sorry to admit this to you
                 Sophia—admit that I truly believe
                 that Africans are our equals. I hope
                 someday I am proven wrong . . . in
                 any case, because I know God has
                 blessed you with good sense and
                 good will, I will withdraw all of my
                 assets from the slave trade and will
                 disentangle myself from this
                 triangle of human misery that I
                 have for too long been a part of.

CONSTANCE.   I have your word as a gentleman.

THOMAS.   No, you have my word as your
                 father. That is of far more value.

CONSTANCE.   Then we shall come home.

SOPHIA.   I got job as sail maker, Mr.
                 Thomas. I can pay rent.

CONSTANCE.   No, Sophia, you are family. You do
                 not have to pay.

THOMAS.   Constance, when God made this
                 world, he did not create it for one
                 as good as you.

CONSTANCE.   Father, it is not God's world that is
              lacking in goodness, it is yours.

SOPHIA.   I'll pack our things.

THOMAS.   I'll send my carriage.

SOPHIA.   Constance, we going home!

(LIGHTS COME DOWN TO END THE SCENE.)

ACT II, SCENE VII

SCENE:	LIGHTS COME UP on CHARLES and ADAM on the after deck of *Rising Sun*. Charles is on the helm; Adam is standing nearby; he cracks a coconut with a machete, opens it, drinks the milk and then splits the shell and begins to dig out the pulp.
ADAM.	You want meat from coconut, Mr. Charles.
CHARLES.	No, thank you, Mr. Adam.
ADAM.	You very quiet tonight, Mr. Charles.
CHARLES.	That is true. There is much on my mind.
ADAM.	I look at chart; we gittin' close now.
CHARLES.	You have become a good sailor, Mr. Adam. You learn very quickly.
ADAM.	When sea not angry; this not bad place to be 'cept for what we doin' here.

CHARLES.   I guess that is what occupies my mind and holds my tongue silent.

ADAM.   Adam thought that it. Almost time you have to decide what path to take.

CHARLES.   We'll make landfall tomorrow . . .

ADAM.   Anguilla.

CHARLES.   Like I said—you learn fast.

ADAM.   Alter course to port to make Saint Thomas . . .

CHARLES.   Or continue west to make Havana in a few days.

ADAM.   You know, Mr. Charles—I been thinkin' too.

CHARLES.   I pray that your thoughts are less troubled than are mine, Mr. Adam.

ADAM.   I think that be so. I havin' *good* thoughts . . . most of the time.

CHARLES.   Would you mind sharing them with me, Mr. Adam?

ADAM.   Not at all, Mr. Charles. (A beat.) What I been thinkin'—is that when we git back Newport and I be free—I thought that—maybe I could go to sea with you again, maybe be on crew of sloop you be captain of. What you think of that?

CHARLES. Mr. Adam, I am honored that I have gained some measure of your trust, and I would consider it a privilege to go to sea with you. However, if I get back to Newport, you will either hate me—or I, in all likelihood, will probably never be in a position to command a ship again. (A few beats.) Do you understand?

(Adam slams the machete into the coconut shell, splitting it in half.)

ADAM. Adam know you do what you have to do; same true for Adam. Hard for both of us.

CHARLES. You have to understand that I have—obligations to many people, not the least of which is Constance's father.

ADAM. Adam under no obligation anymore; could git free in these islands and have Miss Sophia come find me; she have money and free. She go wherever she wants.

CHARLES. That is true.

ADAM. You know where it say in the Bible that—man jist a little lower than the angels?

CHARLES. Yes, and that he is crowned with a crown of glory and honor.

118

Constance has read that passage to me many times.

ADAM.   You think that be true?

CHARLES.   Not for me.

ADAM.   How 'bout those peoples we got below?

CHARLES.   I think, in God's eyes, they are much closer to the angels than are we.

ADAM.   In God's eyes . . . ?

CHARLES.   Yes . . . in God's eyes.

ADAM (waving the machete). You do one thing for Adam, Mr. Charles, 'fore we make huge mistake, 'fore you throws away Miss Constance and I maybe throws my own life away.

CHARLES.   What would you have me do, Mr. Adam?

ADAM.   You go below and look at those peoples; take a lamp and look into their eyes, Mr. Charles. Then you decide how close to the angels you wanna be. You decide then who it is you gots this obligation to. You do that for Mr. Adam.

CHARLES.   Very well. I will do that.

119

ADAM.   Right now you do it! I take the
                        helm.

CHARLES.   Aye, Mr. Adam. I am steering due
                        west.

ADAM.   I knows which way you steering!

(Adam takes the helm; Charles starts below and then stops
and looks up.)

ADAM.   Those peoples only wants what we
                        all wants.

(Charles nods and then goes "below" as Adam remains at
the helm. Adam looks up studying the stars, feeling the
fresh breeze on his face, and takes a huge breath of the
night air. In a moment, low at first, a chant of FREEDOM
starts from below and builds. It grows louder and louder—
FREEDOM, FREEDOM, FREEDOM, FREEDOM and
it continues as Charles emerges from below. He is shaken.

ADAM.   Wind is shifting.

CHARLES.   Aye, wind is shifting.

ADAM.   Which way it blow, Mr. Charles—
                        Havana or Charlotte Amalie?

                        (BLACKOUT.)

ACT II, SCENE VIII

SCENE:

LIGHTS COME UP on CONSTANCE and SOPHIA in the sitting room of the Clarke estate. Both are seated beside an oil lamp, reading separate letters.

CONSTANCE.

Your child will be with you soon, Sophia.

SOPHIA.

God willin'. (A beat.) Yours too.

CONSTANCE.

Not too soon, I hope. (A beat.) It is going to be close.

SOPHIA.

You never tell, Mr. Charles 'bout baby.

CONSTANCE.

No.

SOPHIA.

He gonna be surprised sure enough.

CONSTANCE.

Yes, I should imagine so.

SOPHIA.

But *good* surprise.

CONSTANCE.

I hope so.

SOPHIA.

Adam say he learn to be a good sailor from Mr. Charles; can be partner with him some day. Mr. Charles make him Captain. And we all be friends.

CONSTANCE.

We are friends now, Sophia. You are my dearest friend.

SOPHIA.

And we stay friends, no matter what?

CONSTANCE.

Yes, no matter what. (A beat.) Sophia . . . what is it?

SOPHIA.

Maybe . . . I not such good friend after all.

CONSTANCE.

Sophia—don't be ridiculous, you are like a sister to me.

SOPHIA.

Not very good one.

CONSTANCE.

Sophia—I have never had a better friend. Is something wrong?

SOPHIA.

Maybe—maybe it not good idea for Mr. Charles to get my boy.

CONSTANCE.

What?

SOPHIA.

He maybe not even remember me now; maybe he like it in South Carolina, like his other momma and not want to go away.

CONSTANCE.

He cannot stay there, Sophia. You know what will happen to him.

SOPHIA.   I not want to make any trouble for Mr. Charles.

CONSTANCE.   You didn't make this trouble.

SOPHIA.   Afraid for Adam too. Afraid of what he might do.

CONSTANCE.   Mr. Adam will not do anything. Has he not agreed to raise your son as his own along with whatever other children you may be blessed with?

SOPHIA.   Yes, he say that.

CONSTANCE.   Then there is nothing to be afraid of.

SOPHIA.   No, you not understand.

CONSTANCE.   Then help me to understand.

SOPHIA.   I not tell you truth.

CONSTANCE.   About . . . what?

SOPHIA.   'Bout father of my son.

CONSTANCE.   I see. (A beat.) Do you . . . want to tell me now?

SOPHIA.   I ashamed 'bout it—hard to tell.

CONSTANCE.   Sophia . . . you did no wrong; you were a child.

SOPHIA.   No, you not understand . . . father
                           is not slave. (A beat.) He white.

CONSTANCE.   Oh . . . god . . . please don't tell me
                           that . . .

SOPHIA.   My baby very light too; maybe pass
                           for white.

CONSTANCE.   Sophia—who is the child's father?
                           (Sophia turns away.) You *must* tell
                           me!

SOPHIA (weeping). Can't tell you, Miss Constance.
                           (Begins to run off.) I too ashamed.

CONSTANCE (runs after her). Sophia . . . Sophia

                    (BLACKOUT.)

ACT II, SCENE IX

SCENE:	LIGHTS COME UP on JOHN RUTLEDGE in his shipping office in Charleston, SC. He is shuffling through some papers when CHARLES and ADAM ENTER.
JOHN.	Brother Charles, what an altogether not unexpected surprise. Have your boy wait outside.
CHARLES.	He is not my "boy", Brother. He is my friend.
JOHN.	I know what he is, and I would prefer not to have him in my office. We have business to discuss.
CHARLES.	I will take care of this, Mr. Adam. Wait for me.
ADAM.	I be right here if you be needin' me.
CHARLES.	I will be fine. He is my older brother, but he is no longer my "big" brother. I can take care of this matter.

(ADAM exits.)

JOHN.

I caught wind of your coming, Charles, but didn't know quite what to make of your misadventure in the Indies. What in god's name happened?

CHARLES.

In God's name, I turned over the Africans to the Quakers in Charlotte Amalie.

JOHN.

So . . . it is true.

CHARLES.

It is.

JOHN.

Voluntarily? You—did this voluntarily?

CHARLES.

That is correct, sir.

JOHN.

And being of sound mind and so forth?

CHARLES.

I knew exactly what I was doing.

JOHN.

My god, they got to you, did they not?

CHARLES.

They?

JOHN.

Quakers. Yankees. Your Harvard education. Constance. I don't know. I hope you are aware that you have put me and a number of Mr. Clarke's other investors in a very difficult position, both legally and financially.

A LITTLE LOWER THAN THE ANGELS

CHARLES.
Or you can look at it another way. Legally, and *morally*, which I realize you care little about, I took it upon myself to prevent you from engaging in the illegal practice of slave trading. I think that perhaps I am owed a debt of gratitude.

JOHN.
I think not, Charles. Gratitude is cheap; investing in a ship in the African trade is very costly. And it is clear, that you took it upon yourself to deprive a number of honest men a fair return on their investment.

CHARLES.
Honest men?

JOHN.
More so that a renegade Captain who relinquishes his cargo and then uses his brother's good name to obtain credit to buy sugar and molasses so he won't return home completely empty handed.

CHARLES.
I intend to make good on my obligations, Brother.

JOHN.
Using what for capital?

CHARLES.
My name is not altogether without merit; I think I have retained my honor even if I have disappointed a few investors.

JOHN.

You know nothing of honor; was it honor that motivated you to surrender another man's property?

CHARLES.

As a matter of fact, it was.

JOHN.

Was it honor that drove you to use my name and that of John Clarke to secure credit to buy sugar and molasses?

CHARLES.

No, that was a necessity. And in time, I assure you, that you shall have your money. (A beat.) But that is not what I am doing here. As I am sure that you are aware, I came for something else.

JOHN.

Of course, Brother, this is a social call. Let us retire to the pub and talk of old times. Let us talk of those times when every one of God's creatures knew its rightful place in the great chain of being. Let us depart.

CHARLES.

Not yet, Brother. I will only raise my glass with you after you have relinquished Sophia's son.

JOHN.

Of course, Sophia's son. I had correspondence from your— betrothed—that it was her desire, as well as yours, although you were not there to express it, that the child be returned to his mother.

CHARLES.   That is our wish.

JOHN.   From what I read, it appears that
                  your Constance and the slave girl
                  are growing very close. Imagine
                  that . . .

CHARLES.   Sophia is free, and you need not be
                  concerned with their friendship. It
                  is not your affair. About the boy?

JOHN.   Ah, yes, the boy . . .

CHARLES.   Is there a problem, John? I will do
                  whatever it takes to acquire him.

JOHN.   Is that a threat, Charles, or an offer
                  to purchase my property?

CHARLES.   John, I am no longer a child you
                  can torment, and I have neither the
                  stomach nor the patience for one
                  of your games. I want to go home.
                  Where is the boy?

JOHN.   I have sent for him; he will be here
                  soon enough.

CHARLES.   What must I do to secure the
                  child's freedom?

JOHN.   Nothing.

CHARLES.   I know you better than that, John.

JOHN.   Honestly, you need not do
                  anything. The child is proving to be

something of an inconvenience at best, and at worst, a liability.

CHARLES.   I know not what artifice you are employing, but I will require a document from you before I leave granting the child his freedom.

JOHN (holding up a paper). Done. (A beats.) There is just . . . one thing.

CHARLES.   Of course . . . one thing.

JOHN.   In light of your recent sojourn in Africa and the kinship you obviously feel with your African brethren, you might be dis-appointed to learn that this child is not . . . entirely of African descent.

CHARLES.   Go on . . .

JOHN.   I don't think I have to explain it to you—Brother, as you well know, it is a planter's prerogative to use his property in any way that he sees fit.

CHARLES.   My god, John, tell me you did not—

JOHN.   She was my property; Charlotte had run off to Atlanta and I was probably a little drunk, maybe not, on the first occasion. In any case, she was mine to do with as I pleased.

130

CHARLES.   She was a child!

JOHN.   No! Had she not been a woman, she would not have conceived a child.

CHARLES.   This child is your son?

JOHN.   And your nephew, but he is not in my mind a suitable heir to the Rutledge holdings of 5,000 acres of land, some 300 slaves, and a shipping concern. You are next in line, Charles, or would you prefer I will it to my bastard son?

CHARLES.   It is inconceivable to me that you forced yourself on a child.

JOHN.   And it is inconceivable to me that you could give away another man's property.

CHARLES.   You are a disgrace.

JOHN.   Me! How dare you call *me* a disgrace!

CHARLES.   I put that label on you and every slave owner North and South who has ever taken a Negro woman by virtue of his power over her. You take Negro women, little more than children, at will, and then you place your lust and depravity on the shoulders of Negro men, who, in your minds conspire to desire white women. Where is there honor in such twisted logic and criminal behavior? You are not only a disgrace to yourself and our family but to the human race!

JOHN.   How dare you talk to me of disgrace when as we speak your betrothed is out of shame sequestered in her home in Newport pregnant with your child?

CHARLES (stunned). What?

JOHN (loving it).   You did not know? (A beat.) Everyone from Boston to Barbados knows—knows the shame you have brought on the Clarke name in Newport and the Rutledge in Charleston.

CHARLES.   This cannot be.

JOHN.   If that is the case, Brother, then your betrothed has obviously enjoyed the favors of another man, or men, in your absence.

CHARLES.   Hold your tongue, Brother, or I will rip it from your mouth.

ADAM (entering).   Mr. Charles—Sophia's boy here. He be white!

(Adam starts for John; John takes a pistol from his desk just as Charles reaches Adam and restrains him.)

CHARLES.   Adam, no! He'll kill you!

ADAM.   You take Miss Sophia?

CHARLES.   Adam—ADAM! Let me take care of this. He has insulted me and he has insulted Constance to say nothing of what he has done to Sophia.

ADAM.   He gots to pay!

JOHN.   If you don't want him dead, get him out of here.

CHARLES.   We are going, but first let me have my say. You have insulted me, Brother. You have insulted my fiancée. You have questioned my honor, and you have disgraced the family name.

JOHN.   And what are you going to do about it?

CHARLES.   You leave me no choice but to demand that we settle our differences on a field of honor.

JOHN.   You—you are challenging me to a duel?

CHARLES.   Have you not the courage to face me now that I am your equal in stature?

JOHN.   Pistols make up for a lack of stature, Brother.

133

CHARLES. Then let it be pistols.

JOHN. Twenty paces?

(Charles nods. The number of paces will depend upon the size of the production space. At 20 paces, each actor takes 10 steps away from the other, etc.)

JOHN. Agreed. Sunrise tomorrow.

CHARLES. Sunrise it is.

JOHN. You had best enjoy it, Brother, for it will be the last one your eyes shall ever see.

(BLACKOUT.)

ACT II, SCENE X

SCENE:

LIGHTS COME UP on JOHN RUTLEDGE, CHARLES and ADAM in an "open field" at sunrise the next day. John and Charles are standing back to back and both are holding a pistol. Adam is close to Charles.

ADAM.

You shoot to kill, Mr. Charles. You don't kill him—neither one of us leave this place alive.

CHARLES.

It has come down to this—brother against brother. I know what I must do.

ADAM.

Miss Constance be waitin' for you. Miss Sophia waitin' for me. You aim good, shoot first.

CHARLES.

Move away, Adam and count.

(Adam moves upstage and begins to count paces as the brothers start to pace.)

ADAM.

One, two, three, four, five, six, seven, eight, nine, ten.

(Both men turn and fire. BLACKOUT.)

ACT II, SCENE XI

SCENE: LIGHTS COMES UP on SOPHIA, THOMAS and MARIA in the Clarke home in Newport a week or so later. They are all dressed in mourning clothes, and Sophia is rocking an infant in a crib.

SOPHIA. There, there, baby. Don't you cry now. Miss Sophia takin' good care of you. No need to fret none at all. And your papa be here any minute now. He be here with my boy. You and him be best friends like I was with your momma. Adam be here too. We all be lookin' after you. No need for you to fret now.

THOMAS. You can go, Mrs. Pires. There is nothing more for you to do here.

(Thomas goes over and takes the baby so Sophia can say goodbye to Maria.)

MARIA. I thought maybe I could . . . help . . . . explain—

THOMAS.   There is no explanation—children die for the sins of their fathers. That is all. The fault is mine, not yours. You and Dr. Coddington did all that was humanly possible.

MARIA (goes to Sophia). Sophia, you take time off; settle things here. You excellent sail-maker still. With me you make much monies for your family.

SOPHIA.   Thank you—thank you for job and for taking me and Miss Constance in when . . .

THOMAS.   You need not go into that, but, yes, thank you, Mrs. Pires for your support of Constance and Sophia when, when . . .

MARIA.   You need not go into that. (A beat.) Good-bye, Sophia. You come back when you ready; I keep job for you. Give job to man Adam too if he not want to go sailin' off to ends of earth lookin' for whatever mens lookin' for when they go sailin' off.

(CHARLES and ADAM enter. Maria lets them pass and then exits.)

ADAM.   Miss Sophia!

SOPHIA.   Oh, Mr. Adam! You back at last— at long last.

ADAM (as they embrace). And I gots your boy right here too; Mr. Charles havta shoot his brother to git him, but he here. Right out there in the carriage sound asleep. He done wore out, but he remember you all right. I tells him all 'bout you every day. He remember you foe sure.

SOPHIA (starting out). My baby. My baby.

THOMAS.   Sophia, wait, please! (She stops. Then to Charles.) Charles, this little angel is your daughter.

CHARLES.   I—I have a child?

THOMAS.   A beautiful little girl.

CHARLES (looks, then). A daughter. . . where is Constance?

(Thomas can't answer; he looks away and then to Sophia.)

CHARLES.   Sophia?

SOPHIA.   She gone, Mr. Charles.

CHARLES.   Gone?

SOPHIA.   Gone to God.

CHARLES.   What?

SOPHIA.   God take her away.

CHARLES.   No. That cannot be. No! (A beat.) Thomas—?

THOMAS.   She had a bad time of it, Charles—
                          she hemorrhaged. She left us a few
                          hours ago. We did everything we
                          could.

CHARLES.   No. No! NO!

SOPHIA.   She in a better place now, Mr.
                          Charles.

CHARLES (falling to his knees). Tell me this is not so. I—
                          I did everything right; I did
                          everything God asked of me.

SOPHIA.   And God give you a beautiful child.

CHARLES.   In place of Constance?

SOPHIA (helping him get up). You come now; you come
                          say good-bye to Miss Constance;
                          she waiting for you. I promise her
                          you say good-bye. (A beat.) She be
                          free now, like we all be free. Ain't
                          that so, Mr. Thomas?

THOMAS (distraught). I do not know, Sophia. I do not
                          know.

SOPHIA.   Well, I know I be free. I gots my
                          son and my man. And here we all
                          together, all of us, jist like Miss
                          Constance always tellin' me we be,
                          like family. Mr. Adam here and our
                          beautiful childs. I free. Mr. Adam
                          free. Moses delivering those
                          Africans to freedom. We all free,

same as Miss Constance. Ain't that so, Mr. Adam?

ADAM.   Don't know foe sure, Miss Sophia; mostly it true I think, but . . . in my heart—I not sure any of us truly free—'till we *all* be free.

(They both move close to Charles; Sophia takes his arm. Thomas joins them as they stand together as a family.)

SOPHIA.   Come on now, Mr. Charles. You go in there and say good-bye to Miss Constance. Then we gots much work to do here and back home in Carolina.

(They stand in a pristine white light as we HEAR A VOICE.)

CONSTANCE (off). O Lord, our Lord, how excellent is thy name in all the earth! who hast set thy glory above the heavens. [3] When I consider thy heavens, the work of thy fingers, the moon and the stars, which thou hast ordained; [4] What is man, that thou art mindful of him? and the son of man, that thou visitest him? [5] For thou hast made him a little lower than the angels, and hast crowned him with glory and honour. [6]

(LIGHTS COME DOWN SLOWLY.)

THE END

ABOUT THE AUTHOR

David W. Christner was born in Sweetwater, TN and raised in rural Oklahoma. He attended high school in Mountain View, a small farming community situated between the Washita River and the Wichita Mountains in the southwestern part of the state. As a Commissioned Officer in the U.S. Navy, Christner served three years at sea fighting the Vietnam War and two years ashore in Norfolk, VA. After completing his graduate education at OU, Christner settled in southern Rhode Island and for twenty years worked as a technical writer, editor and multimedia training developer for a variety of defense contractors and hi-tech multinational corporations during the day and wrote plays and novels at night. His stage plays *The Wall, Bui-Doi: The Dust of Life, The Walk, Red Hot Mamas, The Babe, the Bard and the Baron, The Bitch of Bailey's Beach, Ezra and Evil, What About Mimi?,* and *This Blood's for You* have been finalists or winners in national/international playwriting competitions. Speculations on the cosmos, sex, war, religion, injustice, environmental exploitation, aging, women's issues, the homeless, the colonial slave trade and capital punishment have formed the thematic content of the plays and novels he has written so far. His plays have been produced in the U.S., Australia, Japan, Belgium, India, Ghana, England and Canada. Translations of *Red Hot Mamas* are running in Russia, The Republic of Belarus and Italy. Christner is theater critic for the *Newport Mercury* in Newport, RI. *A Little Lower than the Angels* is one of Christner's 20 full-length plays.

Made in the USA
Middletown, DE
24 February 2019